OCCUPATIONAL PSYCHOSIS

OCCUPATIONAL PSYCHOSIS

The Hidden Crisis Beneath Occupational Wellness

GEORGIA LEE ARTS
Founder and Director, Occupational Wellness Institute™

Copyright and Unauthorized Use

Occupational Psychosis: The Hidden Crisis Beneath Occupational Wellness

Published by **Occupational Wellness Institute™ Publishing**.

Canon Designation
This work is designated as **Volume I of the Occupational Wellness Institute™ Canon**.

Canonical designation indicates that this text serves a foundational, diagnostic, and definitional role within a governed body of scholarly work stewarded by the Occupational Wellness Institute™.

Canonical works define phenomena, establish conceptual boundaries, and inform institutional discourse. They do not provide applied methods, practitioner training, certification authority, or commercial frameworks.

Application of concepts introduced herein requires formal education, oversight, and ethical governance through appropriately authorized Occupational Wellness Institute™ pathways.

Library of Congress Cataloging-in-Publication Data

ISBN: 979-8-9941272-6-1 (hardcover)

Permissions and Licensing
For permissions, licensing requests, professional training inquiries, or organizational partnerships, contact:

occupationalwellnessinstitute.org

PUBLISHER'S NOTE

This volume is published by the Occupational Wellness Institute™ as part of its scholarly and professional publishing mandate.

The Occupational Wellness Institute™ exists to advance clarity, integrity, and ethical stewardship within the evolving field of occupational wellness. Its publishing arm serves a specific purpose: to support disciplined inquiry into the systemic, psychological, organizational, and ethical dimensions of work - particularly where prevailing models prove insufficient.

Occupational Psychosis: The Hidden Crisis Beneath Occupational Wellness is issued as a scholarly, diagnostic text. It is intended to contribute to research, policy discussion, institutional reflection, and field-level understanding. It is not designed as a practitioner manual, coaching guide, therapeutic resource, or applied framework.

The Institute recognizes that contemporary occupational wellness discourse has expanded rapidly in response to burnout, disengagement, leadership failure, and workforce instability. This expansion has frequently emphasized individual-level solutions while overlooking structural, identity-based, and authority-driven dynamics within occupational systems. This volume addresses that limitation by introducing and defining a phenomenon situated at the intersection of role identity, power, ethics, and institutional design.

As publisher, the Occupational Wellness Institute™ affirms the following principles:

- That **definition must precede intervention**

- That **systemic harm cannot be resolved through individualization alone**
- That **authority to apply concepts carries ethical responsibility**
- That **fields mature through restraint, not proliferation**

Accordingly, this work is published with explicit scope boundaries. It does not provide methods, tools, certifications, or instructions for application. It does not authorize applied use, professional practice, certification, or commercialization of the concepts discussed. Application, where appropriate, requires formal education, oversight, and ethical governance through authorized institutional pathways. Any applied use of concepts introduced herein requires formal education, oversight, and ethical governance through authorized pathways stewarded by the Institute.

This publication reflects the Institute's commitment to disciplinary rigor, conceptual restraint, and long-term stewardship of the occupational wellness field.

CANON DESIGNATION

This volume is formally designated as part of the **Occupational Wellness Institute™ (OWI) Canon**.

The OWI Canon is a governed body of scholarly work developed to define, examine, and steward concepts related to occupational wellness, authority, ethical responsibility, and institutional design. Canonical designation signifies that a work is **conceptual, diagnostic, and non-operational** in nature, and that it adheres to the governance principles established by the Occupational Wellness Institute™.

Canonical works are distinguished by the following characteristics:

- They define phenomena rather than prescribe interventions
- They establish conceptual boundaries and ethical constraints
- They do not provide methods, tools, certifications, or applied frameworks
- They are not intended for direct professional, therapeutic, or organizational application
- They require formal governance, oversight, and institutional stewardship for any future use

This volume, *Occupational Psychosis: The Hidden Crisis Beneath Occupational Wellness*, is issued as a **canonical text**. Its purpose is to name and clarify a systemic phenomenon and to delineate the ethical conditions under which responsible engagement may occur in the future.

Canonical designation does not imply finality. It signifies disciplinary restraint and institutional responsibility at this stage of the field's development.

Interpretation of this work should remain consistent with the scope, purpose, and ethical boundaries articulated throughout this volume.

STATEMENT OF SCOPE, PURPOSE, AND STEWARDSHIP

This book introduces and defines *Occupational Psychosis* as a systemic phenomenon affecting modern work, leadership, and occupational identity. It is presented as a conceptual, analytical, and scholarly contribution to the fields of occupational wellness, organizational psychology, leadership studies, identity science, and the economics of work.

The purpose of this work is to name, contextualize, and examine a category of occupational harm that has remained largely invisible within existing wellness, leadership development, and professional ethics frameworks.

The term *diagnostic* is used in a systems-level and conceptual sense, referring to pattern recognition and analytical framing, not to assessment, evaluation, or determination of condition in individuals or organizations. This work does not diagnose individuals, organizations, or professions, nor does it function as a clinical, psychological, or medical assessment tool.

This book is not instructional in nature. It does not teach techniques, frameworks, certifications, or applied interventions.

Instead, it establishes a foundational lens for inquiry that is intended to support responsible scholarship, ethical governance, and future institutional discourse.

What This Book Does

This book:

- Defines *Occupational Psychosis* as a role-induced distortion of perception, judgment, ethics, and identity that can emerge within unexamined occupational systems.
- Examines how power, authority, role identity, incentive structures, and professional narratives interact to normalize harmful distortions of reality.
- Draws from identity science, occupational psychology, leadership theory, systems thinking, economics, and organizational behavior to situate Occupational Psychosis as a legitimate occupational risk for scholarly, ethical, and policy-level consideration.
- Provides language, taxonomy, and analytical framing for recognizing systemic breakdowns that conventional wellness and leadership models fail to detect.
- Serves as a field-level analytical contribution, not a personal development guide or applied intervention.

This book exists to illuminate, not to operationalize.

What This Book Does Not Do

This book does not:

- Provide coaching tools, therapeutic techniques, step-by-step methods, or facilitation models
- Offer certification pathways, practitioner credentials, or applied frameworks
- Train readers to diagnose, treat, or remediate individuals or organizations
- Substitute for clinical, legal, psychological, or organizational licensure
- Grant permission to apply, teach, adapt, or commercialize the concepts herein

This includes informal, derivative, embedded, or interpretive use in coaching, consulting, facilitation, training, or advisory services.

Any attempt to extract techniques, models, or applied practices from this text misrepresents the stated scope and authorial intent of this work and undermines ethical use.

On Application, Training, and Ethical Governance

The application of insights related to Occupational Psychosis, whether in leadership, organizational development, occupational wellness, or advisory contexts, requires formal training, oversight, and ethical governance.

Responsible engagement with this domain demands:

- Clearly defined scope of practice
- Institutional accountability structures
- Competency-based education and supervision
- Safeguards against misuse, projection, or ideological distortion
- A commitment to non-pathologizing, non-exploitative, and evidence-informed practice

For this reason, applied use of these concepts is intentionally separated from this text and reserved for structured educational and certification pathways stewarded through appropriate institutional governance.

This stewardship reflects a commitment to ethical use and public protection, not a claim of exclusive ownership over inquiry or discourse.

This separation between definition and application is deliberate and essential.

CANON CROSS-REFERENCE NOTE

This volume forms part of a governed body of scholarly work stewarded by the Occupational Wellness Institute™.

Concepts, terminology, and analytical distinctions introduced in this text may be referenced, expanded, or examined across other canonical works within the Occupational Wellness Institute™ Canon. Such cross-references are intended to deepen understanding, clarify scope, and maintain conceptual coherence across the canon.

Each canonical volume is designed to stand independently. Cross-referencing does not imply sequential dependency, prerequisite knowledge, or applied authority unless explicitly stated within a given work.

No single volume confers permission to apply, teach, operationalize, or commercialize the concepts described herein. Applied use, practitioner training, or institutional implementation where appropriate is governed separately and subject to formal education, oversight, and ethical governance.

Earlier applied works by the author, including *The $2 Trillion Revenue Gap™ How Identity Misalignment is Silently Costing America Trillions and How Identity Alignment Transforms People, Workplaces, and Communities and Dream Journey, Breaking the Dream Barriers™ A Guide to Bridging Identity Gaps in Life and Career*, were published prior to the formal establishment of the Occupational Wellness Institute™ Canon. While these works informed the author's evolving inquiry, they predate the canon's governance structures, and they are not designated as canonical volumes. These works are governed independently and do not carry the scope, authority, constraints, or institutional applicability of this text.

"People know what they do;
frequently they know why they do what they do;
but what they don't know is what what they do does."
- Michel Foucault

CONTENT

Introduction: Why Occupational Wellness Cannot See What Is Breaking It 16

PART I. DEFINING THE PHENOMENON

1. Occupational Psychosis: A Definition 21

1.1 Meaning and Limits of the Term 23

1.2 Distinguishing Systemic Phenomenon from Clinical Diagnosis 24

1.3 Why Naming Precedes Intervention 25

2. Role-Induced Reality Distortion 27

2.1 Occupational Identity and Perception 27

2.2 Authority, Role Fusion, and Impaired Judgment 28

2.3 Narrative Substitution for Reality-Testing 29

3. Identity, Power, and Ethical Drift 31

3.1 Identity Inflation Within Occupational Roles 31

3.2 Moral Licensing and Normalization of Harm 32

3.3 Power as Insulation from Correction 33

PART II. STRUCTURAL AND SYSTEMIC CONDITIONS

4. Occupational Systems That Reward Distortion 37

4.1 Incentives, Metrics, and Performance Illusions 37

4.2 Success Narratives Versus Human Cost 38

4.3 When Outcomes Mask Systemic Harm 39

5. Leadership, Authority, and the Collapse of Reflexivity 41

5.1 Leadership Identity Versus Leadership Function 41

5.2 Echo Chambers and Affirmation Loops 42

5.3 The Absence of Dissent as Risk Factor 43

6. Professional Language as a Vehicle for Harm 45
6.1 Wellness Language and Moral Signaling 45
6.2 Reputational Insulation Through Helping Narratives 46
6.3 The Risk of Unexamined Care Roles 47

PART III. OCCUPATIONAL PSYCHOSIS ACROSS AUTHORITY SYSTEMS

7. Corporate and Organizational Authority 51
7.1 Performance Culture and Identity Fusion 51
7.2 Structural Denial of Systemic Harm 52

8. Public Sector, Government, and Authority-Bearing Institutions ...54
8.1 Bureaucratic Role Insulation 55
8.2 Diffusion of Responsibility 55
8.3 Policy Narratives and Moral Immunity 56

9. Healthcare, Pharmaceutical, and Credentialed Authority Systems 58
9.1 Protocol Dominance Over Judgment 58
9.2 Expertise Narratives and Ethical Drift 59
9.3 Institutional Denial of Iatrogenic Harm 60

10. Nonprofit, Religious, and Meaning-Based Institutions 62
10.1 Moral Authority and Role Sanctification 62
10.2 Dissent as Moral Failure 63
10.3 Care Identities and Accountability Gaps 64

11. Peer-Based Occupational Ecosystems and Entrepreneurial Authority 66
11.1 Social Authority Without Formal Governance 66
11.2 Mimetic Identity Inflation and Extraction 67
11.3 Reputation as Regulatory Mechanism 68

12. Unregulated Professional and Influence-Driven Fields 70
12.1 Authority Without Oversight 70
12.2 Credential Ambiguity and Boundary Collapse 71
12.3 Ethical Drift Through Normalization 72

PART IV. WHY OCCUPATIONAL WELLNESS FAILS TO DETECT IT

13. The Blind Spots of Occupational Wellness Models.............. 76

13.1 Individualization of Systemic Harm 76

13.2 Resilience Narratives and Misplaced Responsibility 77

14. Burnout Is Not the Root Cause 79

14.1 Burnout as Symptom, Not Source 79

14.2 Why Recovery Models Miss Structural Distortion 80

15. Wellness Without Governance 82

15.1 Absence of Scope and Ethics 82

15.2 Good Intentions as Risk Factor 83

PART V. IMPLICATIONS, BOUNDARIES, AND STEWARDSHIP

16. The Cost of Not Naming Occupational Psychosis 87

16.1 Human Cost 87

16.2 Organizational Cost 88

16.3 Societal and Economic Cost 89

17. Why This Book Stops at Definition 91

17.1 The Danger of Premature Application 91

17.2 Restraint as an Ethical Act 92

18. Toward Ethical Governance in Occupational Wellness 94

18.1 Governance as Prerequisite for Care 94

18.2 Institutional Responsibility and the Future of the Field 95

CONCLUSION: From Invisible Harm to Institutional Responsibility 97

Epilogue 99

References 101

Citation Guidance 109

Canon Index 111

About the Author 112

INTRODUCTION: WHY OCCUPATIONAL WELLNESS CANNOT SEE WHAT IS BREAKING IT

Occupational wellness has become a central concern of modern organizations. Rising rates of burnout, disengagement, moral injury, leadership failure, and workforce instability have prompted widespread investment in wellness programs, leadership development initiatives, and resilience-based interventions. Yet despite this expansion, many of the conditions these efforts aim to address persist, intensify, or recur in new forms.

This book begins from a simple observation: something fundamental is being missed.

Prevailing approaches to occupational wellness tend to focus on individuals through stress management, mindset, coping strategies, and behavioral adjustment while leaving the deeper structures of work largely unexamined. Even organizational-level interventions frequently concentrate on culture, engagement, or performance metrics without addressing how occupational roles themselves shape perception, judgment, ethics, and identity. As a result, systemic distortions embedded within occupational systems often remain invisible, normalized, or reframed as personal failure.

Occupational Psychosis names this blind spot.

The term does not describe a clinical disorder, nor does it pathologize individuals or professions. Rather, it identifies a systemic phenomenon in the form of role-induced distortion that can arise when occupational identity, authority, incentives, and institutional narratives converge in ways that impair reality-testing, ethical reflexivity, and accountability. In such conditions, harm may be sustained not through malice or incompetence, but through normalization reinforced by professional language, peer validation, and structural insulation from corrective feedback.

Occupational psychosis is not confined to any single sector. It can emerge within corporate environments, public institutions, healthcare systems, nonprofit and religious organizations, peer-based entrepreneurial ecosystems, and unregulated professional fields. While its manifestations vary, the underlying structure remains consistent as occupational roles become the primary lens through which reality is filtered, defended, and protected, even when evidence of harm is present.

This phenomenon is difficult to detect precisely because it often operates under the appearance of legitimacy. Authority, expertise, service narratives, and moral positioning may obscure distortion rather than reveal it. In many cases, the very roles entrusted with care, leadership, or improvement become the sites where reflexivity collapses. Occupational wellness frameworks that are designed to support human functioning are rarely equipped to recognize this form of systemic identity distortion.

The absence of language matters. What cannot be named cannot be examined, governed, or held accountable.

This volume is therefore diagnostic in purpose. It does not propose interventions, frameworks, or solutions. It does not instruct readers on how to remediate occupational psychosis, nor does it authorize application of the concept in professional practice. Instead, it establishes conceptual clarity where ambiguity has prevailed, offering definition, analytical framing, and cross-sector examination of a phenomenon that existing models fail to detect.

The restraint of this approach is intentional. In fields carrying ethical, psychological, and institutional consequences, premature application constitutes its own risk. Definition must precede intervention. Governance must precede scale. Without these conditions, even well-intentioned efforts may reproduce the very distortions they seek to resolve.

Intended Audience and Use

This book is written for readers engaged in the study, governance, and stewardship of modern work, including scholars and researchers in occupational psychology, organizational studies, leadership, and identity science; institutional leaders and board-level decision-makers; policy thinkers and ethics committees; economists and systems analysts examining workforce dysfunction; and educators and advanced students studying occupational identity and the future of work.

It is intended for readers seeking conceptual clarity, diagnostic language, and disciplined inquiry rather than prescriptive solutions.

This book is not intended for coaches or practitioners seeking tools, marketable frameworks, or personal branding material; for readers looking for step-by-step methods or self-help strategies; or for those intending to apply, simplify, or commercialize diagnostic language without training, supervision, or institutional accountability.

Occupational Psychosis is not a metaphor to be popularized. It is a phenomenon to be examined with care.

The chapters that follow proceed accordingly. Part I defines occupational psychosis and differentiates it from clinical, metaphorical, or purely cultural interpretations. Part II examines the structural conditions that allow such distortions to emerge and persist. Part III explores how occupational psychosis manifests across authority systems, including peer-based and unregulated environments often excluded from formal analysis. Part IV addresses why occupational wellness frameworks frequently fail to detect these dynamics. Part V considers the implications of leaving the phenomenon unnamed and outlines the ethical necessity of governance and stewardship.

This book stops at definition not because the problem is insoluble, but because responsible engagement begins with clarity.

Occupational wellness cannot mature as a field if it remains focused solely on individuals while ignoring the psychological and ethical consequences of occupational systems themselves. By naming occupational psychosis, this work invites a more disciplined, accountable, and institutionally grounded conversation about what work does to those who inhabit it and what must be understood before change is responsibly pursued.

PART I

DEFINING THE PHENOMENON

CHAPTER 1

OCCUPATIONAL PSYCHOSIS: A DEFINITION

The preceding sections established that occupational wellness frameworks frequently fail to detect certain forms of systemic harm because they focus on individual experience while leaving occupational structure largely unexamined. Before analyzing how such harm manifests across sectors, it is necessary to define the phenomenon that this volume names.

Occupational psychosis refers to a systemic, role-induced distortion of perception, judgment, ethics, and identity that can arise within occupational systems. It is not a clinical diagnosis, nor does it describe a psychiatric condition. Rather, it designates a pattern in which occupational roles, authority structures, incentives, and narratives converge in ways that impair reality-testing and ethical reflexivity at the level of the system.

The use of the term *psychosis* is deliberate and bounded. In clinical contexts, psychosis refers to a disruption in the relationship between perception and reality. In an occupational context, the term is employed analogically to avoid pathologizing individuals and to describe how systems can become detached from the realities they affect while continuing to operate under internally coherent justifications. The distortion does not reside in a person alone; it is sustained by the role, reinforced by peers, and normalized by institutional language.

Occupational psychosis emerges most reliably where three conditions intersect, namely identity fusion with role, authority without adequate reflexive constraint, and incentive structures that reward conformity over correction. Under these conditions, individuals may retain technical competence and moral self-concept while losing the capacity, or permission, to question the effects of their actions. Harm becomes reframed as necessity, dissent as disloyalty, and contradiction as threat.

Crucially, occupational psychosis does not require malicious intent. It often develops in environments that are oriented toward service, care, performance, or improvement. The distortion arises not because individuals lack ethics, but because ethical responsibility becomes diffused across systems, obscured by role expectations, and shielded by narratives of legitimacy. Over time, the occupation itself becomes the primary lens through which reality is interpreted and defended.

This distinguishes occupational psychosis from burnout, bias, or ordinary organizational dysfunction. Burnout describes exhaustion in response to chronic stress; bias describes predictable cognitive shortcuts; and dysfunction describes misalignment between goals and outcomes. Occupational psychosis describes something different, which is a collapse of reflexivity within an occupational system, in which the capacity to perceive harm, question authority, or revise narratives is structurally constrained.

Because this phenomenon is systemic, it is often invisible to those operating within it. Language designed to signal competence, care, or virtue can paradoxically reinforce distortion by insulating roles from scrutiny. The more legitimate an occupation appears, the more difficult it may be to detect when its internal logic has diverged from external reality.

Defining occupational psychosis, then, is not an act of accusation. It is an act of clarification. Without such clarity, efforts to improve occupational wellness risk addressing symptoms while leaving the underlying distortion intact. The chapters that follow elaborate this definition by distinguishing occupational psychosis from related constructs and by identifying the structural conditions that allow it to persist.

1.1 Meaning and Limits of the Term

The term *occupational psychosis* is used in this volume with deliberate precision and equally deliberate limitation. It is not intended as a clinical label, nor as a metaphor for individual irrationality or dysfunction. Rather, it functions as a diagnostic descriptor for a systemic condition in which occupational roles, authority structures, and institutional narratives converge to distort perception, judgment, and ethical reflexivity.

In clinical psychology, psychosis denotes a disruption in the relationship between perception and shared reality. That disruption may involve delusions, hallucinations, or disorganized thought. In an occupational context, the term is employed analogically, not diagnostically, to describe how *systems*, not individuals, can lose contact with the external consequences of their actions while maintaining internal coherence and legitimacy. The distortion is collective, role-mediated, and reinforced by organizational language and norms.

This distinction is critical. Occupational psychosis does not imply mental illness, impaired intelligence, or moral deficiency on the part of individuals. On the contrary, it frequently arises in environments populated by competent, well-intentioned, and highly credentialed professionals. What differentiates occupational psychosis from ordinary error or bias is not ignorance, but structural insulation from corrective feedback.

Sociological and organizational research has long demonstrated that systems can generate internally consistent interpretations of reality that diverge from external conditions. As *Niklas Luhmann* observed, social systems tend toward self-referential closure, reproducing their own logic while filtering out disconfirming information. Similarly, *Karl Weick* described how sensemaking processes privilege plausibility over accuracy, especially under conditions of uncertainty or threat.

Occupational psychosis emerges when this closure becomes ethically consequential, when harm, contradiction, or unintended effects are systematically rationalized, minimized, or rendered invisible through occupational identity and role expectations. The term therefore names a failure of reflexivity, not a failure of character.

The limits of the term are equally important. Occupational psychosis does not apply to all occupational dysfunction, nor does it encompass every form of organizational harm. It is not synonymous with corruption, abuse, or incompetence. It refers specifically to situations in which distortion becomes normalized, shielded by legitimacy, and sustained through occupational identity rather than coercion alone.

1.2 Distinguishing Systemic Phenomenon from Clinical Diagnosis

Because the term *psychosis* carries clinical connotations, it is essential to distinguish occupational psychosis clearly from psychiatric diagnosis. This volume does not assess mental states, symptoms, or individual pathology. It makes no claims about cognition, affect, or neurobiology at the individual level. Any attempt to apply the concept diagnostically to people would constitute misuse.

The distinction rests on level of analysis.

Clinical diagnoses operate at the level of the individual organism. Occupational psychosis operates at the level of roles embedded within systems. The unit of analysis is not the person, but the interaction between role, authority, incentive, and narrative. Individuals may enter and exit such systems without exhibiting any psychological impairment, yet the distortion persists because it is structurally maintained.

This distinction aligns with established scholarship on moral disengagement, group dynamics, and institutional behavior. *Albert Bandura* demonstrated how moral disengagement mechanisms allow individuals to participate in harmful actions without perceiving themselves as unethical, particularly when responsibility is diffused or justified by authority. *Irving Janis* documented how groupthink suppresses dissent and critical evaluation in cohesive groups, even among highly intelligent decision-makers.

Similarly, *Hannah Arendt's* analysis of the "banality of evil" underscored how ordinary individuals can participate in systemic harm through role compliance rather than ideological fanaticism. These insights converge on a common theme that harm does not require madness. It often requires only a role that displaces responsibility and a system that rewards compliance.

Occupational psychosis extends this lineage by focusing explicitly on occupational identity. When professional identity becomes fused with moral worth, legitimacy, or social belonging, questioning the role can feel indistinguishable from questioning the self. Under such conditions, reality-testing is not merely discouraged; it becomes psychologically and socially costly.

This is why occupational psychosis is best understood as a systemic risk, not an individual failing. It is also why traditional occupational wellness models, which focus on stress reduction, resilience, or engagement are poorly equipped to detect it. Those models assume that distress signals harm. Occupational psychosis often operates in environments where distress is absent or reframed as dedication, sacrifice, or professionalism.

1.3 Why Naming Precedes Intervention

Naming a phenomenon is not a neutral act. In fields that carry ethical, psychological, and institutional consequences, naming determines what can be examined, governed, and addressed, and what remains invisible.

Occupational psychosis has remained largely unnamed because it occupies an uncomfortable space between disciplines. It is not easily categorized as individual pathology, organizational dysfunction, or cultural bias. As a result, it is frequently misattributed and harm is individualized as burnout, moral injury, or resilience failure; systemic distortion is reframed as culture fit, leadership style, or performance pressure.

This misattribution has consequences. When systemic distortion is treated as individual deficit, interventions target the wrong level. Wellness initiatives proliferate while underlying authority structures, incentive systems, and identity dynamics remain unchanged. Over time, the gap between intention and impact widens, and occupational wellness efforts themselves risk becoming part of the distortion they seek to resolve.

Naming occupational psychosis serves a disciplinary function. It delineates a category of harm that cannot be addressed through individual coping strategies alone. It creates conceptual space for governance, ethics, and institutional accountability. It also establishes boundaries against premature or inappropriate application. Without clear definition, the concept risks dilution, misuse, or instrumentalization.

This is why this volume stops at definition. Intervention without diagnostic clarity risks reproducing distortion under the guise of improvement. As *Edgar Schein* cautioned, efforts to change organizational systems without understanding their underlying assumptions often reinforce existing dynamics rather than transform them.

Naming is therefore not the beginning of action; it is the condition for responsible restraint. It allows scholars, institutions, and practitioners to recognize when a problem exceeds the scope of existing tools and requires new forms of governance.

Having established what occupational psychosis is, and what it is not, the analysis now turns to the mechanism through which the phenomenon most reliably emerges which is the fusion of identity with occupational role. Chapter 2 examines how roles shape perception, how authority alters reality-testing, and how narrative alignment can substitute for reflexivity within occupational systems.

Understanding role-induced reality distortion is essential to understanding why occupational psychosis is not an aberration, but a predictable outcome under certain structural conditions.

CHAPTER 2

ROLE-INDUCED REALITY DISTORTION

Chapter 1 established occupational psychosis as a systemic phenomenon sustained by occupational roles rather than individual pathology. This chapter examines the primary mechanism through which such distortion arises: the shaping of perception through occupational identity.

Occupational roles do more than organize tasks and responsibilities. They structure attention, delimit acceptable interpretations, and assign moral meaning to action. Over time, roles can function as perceptual filters, determining not only what is seen, but what is considered relevant, permissible, or real. When these filters become rigid or insulated from correction, reality-testing erodes not through delusion but through normalization.

Role-induced reality distortion is therefore not an anomaly. It is a predictable outcome of how identity, authority, and narrative operate within occupational systems.

2.1 Occupational Identity and Perception

Occupational identity refers to the extent to which individuals define themselves through their professional role. This identity provides coherence, purpose, and social belonging. It also shapes perception.

Research in social psychology and organizational studies has consistently shown that identity influences what individuals notice, how they interpret information, and which signals they disregard. Roles function as cognitive schemas that organize experience and filter ambiguity. Within occupational systems, these schemas are reinforced by training, evaluation metrics, peer norms, and institutional language.

When occupational identity remains flexible, it can support ethical judgment and adaptability. When it becomes rigid or fused with moral worth, perception narrows. Information that aligns with role expectations is amplified; information that contradicts them is discounted or reframed. Over time, the role becomes not simply something one does, but the primary lens through which reality is interpreted.

This process is not inherently harmful. All roles require selective attention. The risk emerges when occupational identity becomes overdetermining and displaces other sources of meaning, accountability, or perspective. Under such conditions, challenges to the role are experienced as threats to the self, and corrective feedback becomes psychologically costly.

Organizational theorists have long noted this dynamic. *Edgar Schein* described how deeply embedded role assumptions can persist even when they no longer serve the organization's stated goals. Similarly, *Karl Weick* emphasized that sensemaking processes privilege coherence over accuracy, especially when identity is at stake.

In occupational psychosis, identity-driven perception becomes structurally reinforced. The system rewards those who embody the role convincingly and marginalizes those who disrupt its narrative. Distortion thus becomes adaptive within the system, even as it generates harm beyond it.

2.2 Authority, Role Fusion, and Impaired Judgment

Authority intensifies the effects of occupational identity. When roles carry formal or informal authority, the fusion between role and judgment becomes especially consequential.

Authority alters decision-making by redistributing responsibility. Actions taken under the auspices of a role are often experienced as less personal and more obligatory. This diffusion of responsibility can impair ethical reflexivity, particularly when authority is legitimized by institutional narratives of service, expertise, or necessity.

Classic research on obedience and authority demonstrated how individuals defer judgment when acting within sanctioned roles. *Stanley Milgram's* work showed that ordinary individuals would perform actions they otherwise found objectionable when those actions were framed as role requirements. While such findings are often discussed in extreme contexts, their implications for everyday occupational systems are profound.

Role fusion occurs when authority is not merely exercised, but internalized. In such cases, questioning the role feels equivalent to questioning legitimacy itself. Judgment becomes impaired not because individuals lack ethical capacity, but because ethical deliberation is constrained by role expectations and institutional pressure.

This impairment is often invisible from within the system. Authority confers not only power, but credibility. The more authoritative the role, the less likely its assumptions are to be scrutinized. Over time, authority can function as a substitute for reality-testing which shields decisions from external challenges and internal doubt.

Occupational psychosis emerges most readily where authority is combined with identity fusion and weak governance. In such environments, judgment is not suspended; it is redirected inward, toward maintaining role coherence rather than evaluating external impact.

2.3 Narrative Substitution for Reality-Testing

Narratives play a central role in sustaining role-induced distortion. Occupational systems rely on stories to justify action, coordinate behavior, and confer meaning. These narratives can be explicit in the form of mission statements, values, or professional codes. These narratives can be implicit when embedded in language, ritual, and reputation.

Narratives become problematic when they begin to substitute for empirical feedback. Instead of asking whether actions are producing harm, systems ask whether actions align with the narrative. Instead of responding to contradiction, they reinterpret it as misunderstanding, resistance, or threat.

This substitution is particularly powerful in roles associated with care, leadership, or moral authority. Narratives of helping, service, or expertise can insulate roles from scrutiny by framing dissent as disloyal or unethical. *Albert Bandura* noted in his work on moral disengagement that language plays a critical role in sanitizing harm and maintaining moral self-concept.

Narrative substitution does not require deception. It operates through selective attention and framing, privileging coherence over consequence. When narratives dominate, reality-testing becomes secondary to narrative maintenance. Evidence that contradicts the story is minimized while evidence that supports it is amplified.

In occupational psychosis, narratives achieve a self-sealing quality. The system's language explains away its failures while reinforcing its legitimacy. Over time, the distinction between narrative alignment and ethical accountability blurs.

This dynamic helps explain why occupational psychosis can persist even in the absence of overt distress. If the narrative holds, the system appears functional from within, regardless of its external effects.

Role-induced reality distortion explains *how* occupational psychosis takes shape at the level of perception and judgment. The next question is why such distortion is tolerated, normalized, or even rewarded.

Chapter 3 examines the relationship between identity, power, and ethical drift and shows how authority structures and incentive systems can transform distortion from a liability into an asset, and why correction becomes increasingly difficult once that transformation occurs.

CHAPTER 3

IDENTITY, POWER, AND ETHICAL DRIFT

Chapter 2 examined how occupational roles shape perception and judgment through identity, authority, and narrative. This chapter addresses a further question: why do such distortions persist once they emerge? The answer lies in the interaction between identity, power, and ethical self-concept.

Ethical drift rarely announces itself as deviation. It develops incrementally, through processes that preserve moral self-image while altering the criteria by which harm, responsibility, and accountability are assessed. Occupational systems do not abandon ethics; they redefine them in ways that align with role expectations, authority structures, and institutional incentives.

3.1 Identity Inflation Within Occupational Roles

Identity inflation occurs when an occupational role expands beyond its functional boundaries and becomes a primary source of moral worth, legitimacy, or self-definition. The role is no longer something one performs; it becomes who one is.

Occupational identity is necessary for coherence and professional competence. Problems arise when identity becomes overidentified with role authority or mission. In such cases, the role absorbs ethical significance beyond its scope, and actions taken in service of the role are experienced as inherently justified.

Research on identity and organizations has consistently shown that strong identification increases commitment and performance, but also reduces critical distance. *Edgar Schein* noted that deeply internalized role assumptions are among the most resistant elements of organizational culture, persisting even when external conditions change. When identity inflation occurs, questioning the role feels indistinguishable from questioning moral character.

This inflation is often encouraged implicitly. Institutions reward those who embody role ideals convincingly, while marginalizing those who introduce friction or ambiguity. Over time, the system selects individuals whose identity aligns seamlessly with role narratives. Distortion becomes a marker of belonging, not a deviation.

Identity inflation does not require arrogance or narcissism. It frequently develops in roles associated with service, care, leadership, or expertise. The more morally charged the role, the greater the risk that ethical scrutiny is displaced by identity affirmation.

Within occupational psychosis, identity inflation functions as a stabilizer. It binds individuals to roles in ways that make disengagement, dissent, or self-correction psychologically costly even when evidence of harm accumulates.

3.2 Moral Licensing and Normalization of Harm

Moral licensing refers to the process by which prior or perceived moral behavior creates psychological permission for subsequent actions that would otherwise generate ethical concern. Within occupational systems, moral licensing is often embedded in role narratives rather than conscious calculation.

When an occupation is framed as inherently beneficial by serving the public good, protecting others, or improving lives, the actions taken under its banner inherit moral credit by association. This credit can be drawn upon, implicitly, to justify decisions that cause harm or suppress dissent. Harm is not denied and it is reframed as necessary, unavoidable, or justified by higher purpose.

Albert Bandura's work on moral disengagement provides a foundational account of how language and framing facilitate this process. Euphemistic labeling, diffusion of responsibility, and appeals to moral justification allow individuals and groups to maintain a positive self-concept while participating in harmful systems.

Within occupational psychosis, moral licensing becomes structural. It is embedded in job descriptions, performance metrics, and institutional language. Harmful outcomes are normalized not because they are invisible, but because they are rendered morally acceptable within the system's narrative.

This normalization is reinforced socially. Peer validation, professional recognition, and reputational incentives reward alignment with role expectations. Over time, the threshold for ethical concern shifts. What once triggered discomfort becomes routine.

Importantly, moral licensing operates without malice. Individuals often experience themselves as ethical precisely because they are fulfilling their occupational role. This is why ethical drift is difficult to interrupt from within the system. Correction appears as a betrayal of purpose, not as a moral improvement.

3.3 Power as Insulation from Correction

Power magnifies the effects of identity inflation and moral licensing by insulating roles from corrective feedback. Power does not merely enable action; it shapes which signals are received, which voices are heard, and which consequences are acknowledged.

As authority increases, exposure to dissent often decreases. Subordinates self-censor, peers conform, and external critique is filtered through institutional channels. Over time, power generates an echo chamber in which role narratives are continually affirmed and rarely challenged.

Organizational research has repeatedly demonstrated that power alters perception. Those in authority positions are less likely to receive negative feedback and more likely to interpret ambiguous information as supportive of existing assumptions. *Dacher Keltner* and his colleagues have shown that power can reduce empathic accuracy and increase reliance on internal cues over external information.

Within occupational psychosis, power functions as epistemic insulation. The system's internal logic becomes self-validating, while external indicators of harm are discounted as misunderstanding, resistance, or noise. The more insulated the role is, the less incentive exists to revise perception or judgment.

This insulation is often mistaken for confidence, expertise, or leadership strength. Yet it represents a loss of reflexivity in the capacity to examine one's assumptions in light of consequences. Without reflexivity, ethical accountability weakens, even as formal authority remains intact.

Occupational psychosis persists not because correction is impossible, but because the structures that would enable correction are absent or suppressed. Power, when unchecked by governance, becomes a mechanism for sustaining distortion rather than addressing it.

Chapters 1 through 3 established the conceptual foundations of occupational psychosis, including role-induced distortion, identity inflation, moral licensing, and power-based insulation from correction. The analysis now turns from psychological and relational mechanisms to structural conditions.

Chapter 4 examines how occupational systems can actively reward distortion, transforming ethical drift from an unintended consequence into a functional advantage through incentives, metrics, and performance narratives.

PART II

STRUCTURAL AND SYSTEMIC CONDITIONS

Structural and Systemic Conditions

Part I established what occupational psychosis is and how it takes shape through role-induced distortion, identity inflation, moral licensing, and power-based insulation. Part II turns to the structural conditions that allow these dynamics to persist and, in many cases, to be actively rewarded.

Occupational psychosis does not arise in a vacuum. It is cultivated by systems that prioritize measurable outputs over lived impact, narrative coherence over empirical feedback, and short-term performance over long-term integrity. In such systems, distortion becomes adaptive. Ethical reflexivity is costly, while alignment with institutional metrics is rewarded.

This section examines how incentives, metrics, and success narratives can obscure harm, normalize ethical drift, and produce the illusion of effectiveness even as underlying conditions deteriorate. The focus is not on individual intent, but on system design, specifically how organizational structures can convert distortion into a functional advantage.

CHAPTER 4

OCCUPATIONAL SYSTEMS THAT REWARD DISTORTION

Occupational systems translate values into action through incentives and metrics. These mechanisms are not neutral. They shape attention, allocate resources, and determine what counts as success. When poorly aligned with human impact, they can unintentionally reward distortion while penalizing corrective behavior.

This chapter examines how occupational systems can sustain ethical drift by privileging performance indicators that mask underlying harm. The result is a form of institutional success that is internally celebrated and externally legitimized, even as it produces adverse consequences for individuals, communities, and the system itself.

4.1 Incentives, Metrics, and Performance Illusions

Incentives and metrics are essential tools for organizational coordination. They provide clarity, comparability, and accountability. However, when metrics become proxies for reality rather than indicators of it, they can generate performance illusions, signals of success that diverge from actual outcomes.

Research in organizational sociology and economics has long noted that what gets measured tends to drive behavior. Yet measurement systems are necessarily selective. They capture what is easily quantifiable while excluding complex, long-term, or relational effects. Over time, organizations adapt to the measurement regime rather than the underlying purpose it was meant to serve.

This dynamic is exacerbated when incentives are tightly coupled to narrow performance indicators. Individuals and units learn to optimize for metrics even when doing so undermines broader goals. The system appears to function well because targets are met and dashboards remain green while unmeasured costs accumulate elsewhere.

Such conditions create fertile ground for occupational psychosis. Distortion is not only tolerated, but it is structurally reinforced. Questioning the adequacy of metrics threatens perceived competence and legitimacy. Corrective feedback that cannot be easily quantified is discounted or ignored.

As *Donald T. Campbell* famously observed, the more a quantitative indicator is used for decision-making, the more it is subject to corruption pressures and the more it distorts the processes it is intended to monitor. In occupational systems, this distortion can become normalized as "efficiency" or "performance."

4.2 Success Narratives Versus Human Cost

Metrics alone do not sustain distortion; narratives give them meaning. Success narratives translate performance indicators into stories of progress, impact, and legitimacy. These narratives are powerful because they align identity, morale, and public perception.

Success narratives tend to emphasize growth, achievement, and positive outcomes. The human costs of burnout, moral injury, attrition, and collateral harm are reframed as unfortunate side effects, individual weaknesses, or transitional challenges. Over time, the narrative of success becomes self-protective by filtering out information that contradicts it.

This narrative insulation is particularly strong in occupations associated with service, care, or moral purpose. When success is framed as inherently beneficial, acknowledging harm threatens not only reputation but moral identity. As a result, systems develop sophisticated ways of narrating around harm without denying it outright.

Organizational theorists have noted that cultures of success can suppress learning by discouraging acknowledgment of failure. *Amy C. Edmondson's* work on psychological safety highlights how fear of reputational damage inhibits honest reporting of problems. In the absence of safety, success narratives harden into dogma.

Within occupational psychosis, success narratives function as ethical cover. They allow systems to continue harmful practices while maintaining a positive self-image. The greater the narrative coherence, the less visible the human cost becomes.

4.3 When Outcomes Mask Systemic Harm

A defining feature of occupational psychosis is the misalignment between outcomes and impact. Systems may achieve their stated objectives of profitability, efficiency, compliance, and growth while producing harm that remains unaddressed because it falls outside the evaluative frame.

This misalignment is not accidental. It reflects structural choices about what counts as an outcome and whose experience is considered relevant. When outcomes are narrowly defined, systemic harm can be rendered invisible or statistically insignificant.

For example, the high retention of clients, students, patients, or members may be celebrated as success even when the quality of experience deteriorates. Short-term gains may obscure the long-term erosion of trust, well-being, or institutional legitimacy. By the time harm becomes undeniable, it is often attributed to external factors rather than system design.

Systems thinking scholars have emphasized that delayed feedback and complex causality make systemic harm difficult to trace. *Peter Senge* noted that organizations often struggle to see the consequences of their actions because cause and effect are separated in time and space. In such contexts, outcomes that appear positive can coexist with deep structural damage.

Occupational psychosis persists when systems interpret outcomes as proof of correctness rather than prompts for inquiry. The appearance of success becomes a substitute for ethical evaluation. Correction is deferred, rationalized, or dismissed until systemic harm reaches crisis proportions.

Chapter 4 has shown how occupational systems can reward distortion through incentives, metrics, and success narratives that mask harm. The next step is to examine who holds authority within these systems and how leadership structures shape reflexivity.

Chapter 5 turns to leadership, authority, and the collapse of reflexive capacity by exploring how power dynamics and affirmation loops further entrench occupational psychosis by insulating decision-makers from corrective signals.

CHAPTER 5

LEADERSHIP, AUTHORITY, AND THE COLLAPSE OF REFLEXIVITY

Part II has shown how occupational systems can reward distortion through incentives, metrics, and success narratives. This chapter examines how leadership structures interact with those systems to determine whether distortion is corrected or consolidated. The central concern is reflexivity, the capacity of leaders and leadership systems to examine assumptions, receive corrective signals, and revise action in light of consequences.

Reflexivity is not a personality trait. It is a system property, shaped by role design, authority gradients, information flow, and cultural norms. When leadership identity eclipses leadership function, reflexivity collapses. Occupational psychosis then becomes self-reinforcing, sustained not only by structure but by the social dynamics of authority itself.

5.1 Leadership Identity Versus Leadership Function

Leadership function refers to the responsibilities a role is meant to perform, including sensemaking under uncertainty, ethical judgment, coordination, and accountability. Leadership identity refers to how the role is experienced and narrated by the individual, peers, and the institution.

Problems arise when leadership identity becomes detached from leadership function. In such cases, occupying the role is treated as evidence of competence, legitimacy, or moral authority, regardless of outcomes. The role confers status and protection, while functional performance becomes secondary.

Organizational scholarship has long distinguished between role occupancy and role effectiveness. *Edgar Schein* noted that leadership roles can become carriers of cultural assumptions that persist even when they undermine organizational purpose. When identity dominates function, leaders are rewarded for appearing aligned with institutional values rather than for interrogating their effects.

This identity-function gap narrows the space for reflexivity. Leaders become guardians of narrative coherence rather than stewards of learning. Information that threatens identity by implying error, harm, or misalignment is experienced as destabilizing and therefore resisted.

Within occupational psychosis, leadership identity operates as a stabilizing force. It maintains internal order while inhibiting adaptation. The more identity is valorized, the more costly it becomes to revise judgment, even in the face of contrary evidence.

5.2 Echo Chambers and Affirmation Loops

Authority shapes not only decision rights but information environments. As leaders ascend within occupational systems, they are increasingly surrounded by affirming signals of agreement, validation, selective reporting, and reputational reinforcement. These dynamics create echo chambers in which beliefs circulate and intensify without meaningful challenge.

Echo chambers are not merely social phenomena; they are structural outcomes of hierarchy. Subordinates learn which messages are welcomed and which are risky. Peers converge around shared interpretations to maintain cohesion. Over time, dissent is filtered out long before it reaches decision-makers.

Research on power and cognition demonstrates that authority alters attention and perception. *Dacher Keltner* and his colleagues showed that power increases reliance on internal states while reducing sensitivity to external cues. In leadership contexts, this translates into affirmation loops in which leaders act, receive confirmation, and interpret that confirmation as evidence of correctness.

These loops are reinforced by performance metrics and success narratives that were discussed in Chapter 4. When outcomes appear positive, affirmation intensifies; when outcomes are ambiguous, interpretation defaults to identity-protective explanations. The system becomes increasingly self-referential.

Within occupational psychosis, echo chambers do not require deception. They arise from alignment incentives. Individuals who mirror leadership assumptions advance; those who disrupt them exit or are marginalized. Over time, the leadership system loses contact with disconfirming reality while remaining internally coherent.

5.3 The Absence of Dissent as Risk Factor

Dissent is often treated as a cultural preference or interpersonal challenge. In reality, it is a risk management function. The absence of dissent is not a sign of alignment; it is a warning indicator.

High-reliability research has shown that organizations operating in complex, high-stakes environments depend on the ability to surface anomalies and challenge assumptions. *Karl Weick* emphasized that sensitivity to operations and preoccupation with failure are essential for sustained performance. Where dissent is suppressed, learning stalls.

The absence of dissent becomes especially dangerous when leadership identity is moralized. In such contexts, disagreement is reframed as disloyalty, negativity, or ethical deficiency. Silence then appears as virtue, and conformity as commitment. The system mistakes compliance for cohesion.

Occupational psychosis is sustained when dissent is structurally discouraged through formal policy, informal norms, or reputational consequences. Leaders may sincerely believe that dissent is unnecessary because it is no longer visible. The system appears calm precisely because corrective signals have been filtered out.

Importantly, the absence of dissent does not imply consensus. It indicates exit, disengagement, or self-censorship. By the time harm becomes undeniable, the system has lost the internal capacity to respond adaptively. Crisis replaces correction.

Chapters 4 and 5 have shown how occupational systems and leadership structures can reward distortion and suppress reflexivity. The analysis now turns to the subtler mechanism of language.

Chapter 6 examines how professional and wellness language can function as a vehicle for harm by sanitizing distortion, signaling virtue, and insulating roles from scrutiny even as ethical consequences accumulate.

CHAPTER 6

PROFESSIONAL LANGUAGE AS A VEHICLE FOR HARM

Language does not merely describe occupational reality; it organizes it. Professional language establishes what can be named, what can be questioned, and what must remain implicit. In occupational systems, language functions as both a coordination tool and a moral signal, shaping perception long before decisions are made.

This chapter examines how professional and wellness language can become a vehicle for harm when it substitutes moral signaling for ethical accountability, reputation for evidence, and intention for impact. The focus is not on misuse of words by individuals, but on how entire vocabularies can drift from descriptive clarity into protective abstraction.

When language shields roles from scrutiny rather than illuminating consequences, occupational psychosis is not merely sustained, it is legitimized.

6.1 Wellness Language and Moral Signaling

Wellness language emerged to address genuine human need, including stress, burnout, disengagement, and moral injury within modern work. Over time, however, this language has expanded beyond descriptive function into moral signaling, a way for institutions and professionals to demonstrate care, alignment, and virtue without necessarily altering underlying conditions.

Moral signaling occurs when language emphasizes values, intentions, or commitments in ways that displace evaluation of outcomes. Statements about well-being, support, and resilience signal ethical concern while leaving power structures, incentives, and role expectations intact. The presence of wellness language becomes evidence of ethical engagement, regardless of its effects.

This dynamic is not deceptive; it is adaptive. Language that affirms shared values reduces conflict, preserves legitimacy, and sustains identity coherence. Yet when moral signaling replaces ethical inquiry, it obscures harm rather than addressing it.

Scholars of organizational communication have long noted that language can function ideologically by framing reality in ways that protect existing arrangements. *Michel Foucault* argued that discourse both produces and constrains what can be known. In occupational systems, wellness discourse can delimit critique by positioning concern as already addressed.

Within occupational psychosis, wellness language becomes self-referential. It reassures the system of its goodness while insulating it from examining whether its actions align with its stated values. The more fluent the language of care, the harder it becomes to name care's absence.

6.2 Reputational Insulation Through Helping Narratives

Helping narratives are particularly powerful forms of professional language. They frame occupational roles as inherently benevolent and morally justified. When an occupation is defined by activities such as educating, healing, serving, or protecting, critique becomes ethically fraught.

Reputational insulation occurs when helping narratives shield roles and institutions from accountability. Actions taken under the banner of service inherit moral legitimacy, even when they produce harm. The question shifts from what is happening to what is intended.

This dynamic has been documented across sectors. Sociological studies of professions emphasize how moral authority can function as a form of symbolic capital, protecting occupations from external scrutiny. *Pierre Bourdieu* described how symbolic power operates through recognition and legitimacy rather than force. In helping professions, symbolic power often substitutes for empirical evaluation.

Reputational insulation intensifies when professional communities regulate themselves. Peer affirmation reinforces helping narratives, while dissent is reframed as misunderstanding or hostility toward the mission. Over time, reputation becomes both currency and armor.

Within occupational psychosis, helping narratives transform ethical questions into loyalty tests. To question outcomes is to question intent; to question intent is to question identity. Harm is not denied and it is contextualized, minimized, or deferred in the name of the greater good.

6.3 The Risk of Unexamined Care Roles

Care roles, those oriented toward support, healing, guidance, or development, carry heightened ethical responsibility precisely because they involve asymmetric power. Clients, patients, students, or beneficiaries are structurally positioned as recipients of expertise and authority.

The risk emerges when care roles go unexamined. When assumptions about benevolence replace scrutiny, care can become coercive, extractive, or misaligned without appearing so. Good intentions obscure impact.

Psychological and organizational research has shown that moral certainty increases the risk of ethical blind spots. *Jonathan Haidt's* work on moral intuition suggests that individuals often reason post hoc to justify actions aligned with their moral identity. In care roles, moral identity is central, making self-correction particularly difficult.

Unexamined care roles are especially vulnerable to occupational psychosis because they combine moral authority, identity fusion, and narrative insulation. The system experiences itself as ethical by definition, reducing the likelihood that corrective signals will be recognized or acted upon.

This does not imply that care roles are inherently harmful. It underscores the necessity of external governance, reflexive constraint, and disciplined language. Without these, care becomes a site where distortion can persist under the guise of virtue.

Chapters 4 through 6 have examined how occupational psychosis is sustained through structures, leadership dynamics, and professional language. These mechanisms operate across sectors, but they do not manifest identically in every context.

Part III turns from mechanism to manifestation. It examines how occupational psychosis appears across different authority systems that span corporate, governmental, healthcare, religious, peer-based, and unregulated professional environments and reveals how structural distortion adapts to local conditions while maintaining a consistent underlying pattern.

PART III

OCCUPATIONAL PSYCHOSIS ACROSS AUTHORITY SYSTEMS

Parts I and II established the mechanisms and structures through which occupational psychosis emerges and persists. Part III examines how these dynamics manifest across distinct authority systems. While the underlying pattern of role-induced distortion that is sustained by identity, power, incentives, and language remains consistent, its expression varies according to how authority is organized, legitimized, and enforced.

Authority systems differ in their sources of legitimacy (market performance, legal mandate, expertise, moral purpose, peer recognition), yet each creates conditions under which perception can narrow and reflexivity can erode. By examining these systems comparatively, this section clarifies that occupational psychosis is not sector-specific; it is structure-specific.

This chapter begins with corporate and organizational authority, not because it is uniquely problematic, but because it is often treated as the default model of work. Its assumptions about performance, success, and identity shape contemporary occupational life far beyond the corporate sector itself.

CHAPTER 7

CORPORATE AND ORGANIZATIONAL AUTHORITY

Corporate and organizational environments provide a clear illustration of how occupational psychosis can arise within systems that are oriented toward efficiency, growth, and performance. These systems are typically governed by formal hierarchies, quantified objectives, and cultural narratives that equate success with measurable outcomes.

Within such contexts, authority is legitimated primarily through performance. This legitimacy confers power, shapes identity, and determines which signals are amplified or ignored. When performance culture becomes the dominant organizing principle, distortion can emerge not despite success, but because of how success is defined and rewarded.

7.1 Performance Culture and Identity Fusion

Performance culture centers organizational identity on targets, metrics, and competitive outcomes. It provides clarity and coordination, but it also encourages identity fusion through the alignment of personal worth with organizational success and role performance.

As performance indicators become proxies for value, individuals internalize the organization's evaluative logic. Achievement signals competence and failure signals deficiency. Over time, the role ceases to be merely functional and becomes existentially salient. To perform is to belong; to question performance criteria is to risk exclusion.

Research in organizational psychology has shown that strong identification with organizational goals increases motivation and cohesion, but it also reduces critical distance. *Edgar Schein* noted that cultures built around performance assumptions tend to reproduce those assumptions even when they undermine stated values. Identity fusion intensifies this effect by tying personal legitimacy to organizational outcomes.

Within occupational psychosis, performance culture narrows perception. Information that threatens performance narratives such as ethical concerns, unintended consequences, or human costs is reframed as inefficiency, resistance, or noise. The system rewards those who align with performance logic and marginalizes those who complicate it.

This does not require coercion. It operates through aspiration and belonging. Individuals learn, often implicitly, that success depends on embodying the performance identity convincingly. Distortion becomes adaptive and reflexivity becomes risky.

7.2 Structural Denial of Systemic Harm

Corporate and organizational systems are particularly susceptible to structural denial, the systematic minimization or displacement of harm through organizational design rather than explicit intent. Denial operates not by rejecting evidence, but by routing it away from decision-making channels.

Harms that do not register on performance metrics are deprioritized. Long-term consequences are discounted relative to short-term gains. Responsibility is distributed across departments, processes, and roles, making accountability diffuse. As a result, no single actor appears responsible, even when harm is persistent.

Organizational scholars have described this phenomenon as a consequence of complex systems with delayed feedback. *James G. March* observed that organizations often learn from success while ignoring failure, particularly when success reinforces existing identities and power structures. In such environments, outcomes that appear positive can mask accumulating systemic damage.

Structural denial is reinforced by governance mechanisms that prioritize compliance over inquiry. As long as procedures are followed and targets are met, ethical questions are treated as external to performance. The system experiences itself as functioning correctly, even as trust erodes, burnout spreads, or downstream harm intensifies.

Within occupational psychosis, structural denial becomes normalized. The organization does not see itself as causing harm; it sees harm as incidental, unavoidable, or outside its remit. Correction is deferred until crisis forces recognition, often too late for meaningful adaptation.

Corporate and organizational authority illustrates how performance-based legitimacy can fuse identity with outcomes and structurally deny harm. The next chapter examines a different configuration of authority in the public sector, government, and authority-bearing institutions, where legitimacy derives not from market performance but from legal mandate and public purpose.

Chapter 8 explores how bureaucratic roles, policy narratives, and diffusion of responsibility create distinct, but equally potent, conditions for occupational psychosis.

CHAPTER 8

PUBLIC SECTOR, GOVERNMENT, AND AUTHORITY-BEARING INSTITUTIONS

Public sector and policy institutions operate under a distinct configuration of authority. Unlike corporate systems, where legitimacy is largely derived from performance outcomes, government authority is grounded in legal mandate, procedural legitimacy, and public purpose. In this chapter, public-sector and policy institutions are understood to include civilian government bodies as well as state-authorized authority systems, such as the military and law enforcement, where occupational roles are formalized, hierarchical, and ethically consequential. This configuration produces unique strengths in stability, continuity, and rule-based governance, but it also introduces specific vulnerabilities to occupational psychosis.

In public institutions, authority is exercised through bureaucratic roles that are intentionally bound, standardized, and insulated from individual discretion. These features are designed to protect against arbitrariness and abuse. Yet when combined with scale, complexity, and political pressure, they can also suppress reflexivity and obscure responsibility. Occupational psychosis in public systems emerges not through profit-driven distortion, but through procedural rationality detached from lived consequence.

8.1 Bureaucratic Role Insulation

Bureaucratic systems are structured to separate roles from people. Decisions are made according to rules, policies, and standardized procedures rather than individual judgment. This separation is a defining feature of modern governance, intended to ensure fairness, predictability, and continuity.

However, bureaucratic role insulation can also limit ethical reflexivity. When roles are narrowly defined and procedurally constrained, individuals experience their actions as functionally necessary rather than morally discretionary. Responsibility is framed as compliance with process rather than an evaluation of the outcome.

Classic sociological accounts of bureaucracy emphasized this tension. *Max Weber* described rational-legal authority as efficient and impartial yet warned that it could produce an "iron cage" in which procedural rationality displaces substantive judgment. In such systems, legitimacy flows from adherence to rules rather than responsiveness to impact.

Within occupational psychosis, bureaucratic role insulation becomes a stabilizing mechanism. Individuals perform their designated functions competently while remaining insulated from the cumulative effects of those functions. Harm is not denied; it is reassigned to policy, to mandate, to process.

This insulation is reinforced structurally. Appeals to discretion are often discouraged, as deviation from procedure introduces risk. Over time, ethical concern is reframed as overreach, and reflexivity is interpreted as inefficiency. The system functions smoothly precisely because it discourages questioning beyond role boundaries.

8.2 Diffusion of Responsibility

Public sector systems are characterized by distributed authority. Decisions are made through layered processes involving multiple actors, departments, and oversight mechanisms. While this diffusion is intended to prevent unilateral misuse of power, it can also dilute accountability.

Diffusion of responsibility occurs when no single actor experiences ownership over outcomes. Each role contributes a small part to a larger process, making it difficult to trace causality or assign ethical responsibility. Individuals may act with integrity within their role while the system as a whole produces harm.

Psychological research on responsibility diffusion has long demonstrated that shared accountability reduces perceived obligation to intervene. *John Darley* and *Bibb Latané* showed that individuals are less likely to act when responsibility is distributed among many. In bureaucratic systems, this effect is institutionalized.

Occupational psychosis emerges when diffusion becomes normalized. Harmful outcomes are acknowledged but framed as emergent properties of complex systems rather than consequences requiring correction. Each actor can plausibly claim limited agency, even as the system continues unchanged.

This dynamic is exacerbated by scale. Large public institutions often operate at a distance from those affected by their decisions. Feedback is delayed, abstracted, or mediated through data rather than lived experience. As a result, ethical signals weaken as they move upward through the system.

8.3 Policy Narratives and Moral Immunity

Policy institutions rely heavily on narratives of public good to legitimate authority. These narratives are essential for democratic governance, providing justification for collective action and resource allocation. However, they can also produce moral immunity when invoked to shield policy from scrutiny.

Policy narratives frame actions as necessary, evidence-based, or in the service of collective welfare. When outcomes are contested or harmful, critique is often reframed as political opposition, ignorance, or resistance to progress. The moral authority of the policy substitutes for evaluation of its effects.

Political theorists have noted that modern governance often operates through abstraction, translating lived experience into categories, indicators, and models. *James C. Scott* argued that state systems tend to "see" society through simplified schemas that facilitate control while obscuring local knowledge and unintended consequences.

Within occupational psychosis, policy narratives function as ethical closure. The system experiences itself as morally justified by intent and mandate, reducing sensitivity to evidence that contradicts its self-concept. Correction is delayed until failure becomes visible at scale, often after significant harm has occurred.

Importantly, moral immunity does not require bad faith. It arises from the structural alignment of authority, narrative, and legitimacy. The stronger the policy mandate, the more difficult it becomes to question its effects without appearing to challenge the public good itself.

Public sector institutions demonstrate how legal mandate, procedural legitimacy, and policy narratives can insulate systems from reflexive correction. The next chapter examines a different configuration of authority in healthcare, pharmaceutical, and credentialed professional systems, where legitimacy derives from expertise, scientific authority, and professional certification.

Chapter 9 explores how credentialed authority shapes perception, judgment, and accountability and how occupational psychosis can emerge even within systems explicitly designed to heal and protect.

CHAPTER 9

HEALTHCARE, PHARMACEUTICAL, AND CREDENTIALED AUTHORITY SYSTEMS

Healthcare and pharmaceutical systems derive legitimacy from expertise. Authority is grounded in formal training, credentialing, licensure, and adherence to scientific standards. These features are designed to protect patients and ensure reliability at scale. They also create distinctive vulnerabilities to occupational psychosis.

In credentialed systems, authority is conferred not only by role but by knowledge claims. Decisions are justified through protocols, evidence hierarchies, and professional consensus. When functioning well, these mechanisms reduce arbitrariness and error. When they become rigid or insulated from feedback, they can suppress judgment, normalize ethical drift, and obscure harm, even in systems explicitly oriented toward care.

9.1 Protocol Dominance Over Judgment

Protocols are central to modern healthcare and pharmaceutical practice. They standardize care, reduce variability, and translate evidence into action. Protocolization is a rational response to complexity. However, when protocols dominate judgment rather than inform it, clinical reasoning is displaced by procedural compliance.

Protocol dominance occurs when adherence becomes the primary indicator of competence and legitimacy. In such environments, deviation, even when warranted by context, carries professional risk. Judgment is reframed as liability and discretion as error. Over time, practitioners learn that safety lies in following protocol rather than in evaluating outcomes.

Sociological analyses of professions have long noted this tension. *Eliot Freidson* described how professional authority oscillates between autonomy and standardization, with increasing bureaucratization shifting control from practitioners to systems. When protocols become proxies for ethical responsibility, the system experiences itself as safe by definition.

Within occupational psychosis, protocol dominance narrows perception. Harm that occurs within protocol parameters is interpreted as unfortunate but acceptable and harm that challenges protocol assumptions is harder to register. Reflexivity is constrained not by ignorance, but by institutionalized risk management.

9.2 Expertise Narratives and Ethical Drift

Credentialed systems rely on narratives of expertise to legitimate authority. Expertise narratives emphasize training, specialization, and evidence-based practice. They are essential for trust, yet they can also foster ethical drift when expertise becomes a shield against scrutiny.

Ethical drift occurs when confidence in expertise substitutes for ongoing evaluation of impact. The system's self-concept as scientific and rigorous can obscure the possibility that harm is being produced through accepted practices. Questioning outcomes is reframed as questioning expertise itself.

Philosophers of science have emphasized that scientific knowledge is provisional and context-dependent. *Thomas S. Kuhn* showed how paradigms shape what is seen as evidence and which anomalies are ignored. In credentialed systems, paradigms are reinforced by training pipelines, professional bodies, and regulatory alignment.

Within occupational psychosis, expertise narratives become self-sealing. Disconfirming evidence is treated as noise, outlier, or misuse rather than as a signal requiring systemic reassessment. Ethical concerns are deferred to committees, guidelines, or future research, while practice continues unchanged.

This dynamic does not require bad faith. It emerges from the convergence of authority, identity, and institutional incentives. The more invested a system is in its expertise narrative, the more difficult it becomes to acknowledge its limits.

9.3 Institutional Denial of Iatrogenic Harm

Iatrogenic harm, harm caused by intervention, is an acknowledged risk in healthcare and pharmaceutical systems. Yet acknowledging its existence does not ensure its institutional visibility. Occupational psychosis emerges when systems recognize iatrogenic risk abstractly while denying or minimizing it structurally.

Institutional denial operates through categorization and attribution. Harm is classified as rare, acceptable, or attributable to individual error rather than system design. Reporting mechanisms exist, but feedback loops are slow, fragmented, or filtered. As a result, patterns remain obscured even as incidents accumulate.

Public health scholars have noted that large-scale systems often struggle to integrate adverse outcomes into decision-making. *Ivan Illich* argued that professionalized systems can generate harm while framing that harm as the cost of progress. More recent analyses emphasize how data aggregation and risk-benefit models can distance institutions from lived experience.

Within occupational psychosis, institutional denial is reinforced by legitimacy. The system's orientation toward care creates moral insulation, making it difficult to confront harm without threatening identity. Correction is deferred to future innovation rather than present accountability.

The result is a paradox in which systems designed to heal can become structurally incapable of seeing the harm they produce, not because they reject evidence, but because their authority structures filter it out.

Healthcare and pharmaceutical systems illustrate how credentialed authority and expertise narratives can constrain reflexivity even within care-oriented institutions. The next chapter examines a different configuration of moral authority in nonprofit, religious, and meaning-based institutions, where legitimacy is derived less from formal expertise and more from ethical purpose, service, and shared values.

Chapter 10 explores how moral authority and meaning-making can similarly insulate roles from scrutiny, often with profound consequences for accountability.

CHAPTER 10

NONPROFIT, RELIGIOUS, AND MEANING-BASED INSTITUTIONS

Nonprofit, religious, and meaning-based institutions occupy a distinctive position among authority systems. Their legitimacy is derived less from market performance, legal mandate, or technical expertise than it is from moral purpose, service, and shared meaning. These institutions often exist to address suffering, injustice, or existential need which are functions that confer profound ethical authority.

This moral authority is both a strength and a vulnerability. While it can motivate altruism and collective care, it can also create conditions in which occupational psychosis emerges through role sanctification, moral insulation, and weakened accountability. In such systems, distortion is rarely framed as error or failure; it is more often reframed as faithfulness to mission.

10.1 Moral Authority and Role Sanctification

Role sanctification occurs when occupational roles are imbued with moral or spiritual significance that exceeds their functional scope. In nonprofit and religious contexts, roles are often associated with service, sacrifice, calling, or vocation. These associations confer legitimacy and trust, but they can also shield roles from scrutiny.

When roles are sanctified, actions taken within them are presumed ethical by virtue of intent or mission alignment. The role itself becomes a marker of goodness. Questioning decisions, practices, or outcomes can therefore feel like questioning moral integrity rather than organizational effectiveness.

Sociologists of religion and moral institutions have long observed how sacred meanings can attach to social roles. *Émile Durkheim* described how collective ideals become sacralized, transforming social functions into moral absolutes. In organizational contexts, this sacralization can migrate from belief systems to occupational identities.

Within occupational psychosis, role sanctification narrows ethical inquiry. Harm is not denied, but it is reframed as sacrifice, misunderstanding, or necessary suffering in the service of a higher good. The system experiences itself as morally anchored even as its accountability weakens.

10.2 Dissent as Moral Failure

In meaning-based institutions, dissent often carries moral weight. Because authority is justified by purpose rather than procedure, disagreement can be interpreted as misalignment with values, lack of faith, or failure of commitment.

This framing transforms dissent from a functional signal into a character judgment. Those who raise concerns risk being labeled divisive, ungrateful, or insufficiently aligned with the mission. As a result, dissent becomes costly, both socially and morally.

Political and organizational theorists have noted that moralized authority systems are particularly vulnerable to this dynamic. *Hannah Arendt* emphasized that when moral certainty replaces judgment, ethical reflection collapses into rule-following or belief affirmation. Similarly, *Philip Selznick* observed that institutions founded on ideals can drift toward self-protection when ideals become identity markers rather than guiding principles.

Within occupational psychosis, dissent is reframed as threat. Silence appears as virtue and compliance appears as faithfulness. The system loses access to corrective signals precisely because it interprets moral alignment as proof of correctness.

This dynamic is particularly difficult to interrupt because it operates through shared values rather than coercion. Individuals often self-censor out of loyalty and internalize the belief that raising concerns would betray the mission they care about.

10.3 Care Identities and Accountability Gaps

Nonprofit and religious institutions frequently organize around care identities, roles defined by compassion, service, guidance, or healing. These identities create asymmetric power relationships, in which one party is positioned as a helper and the other as a recipient of care.

Care identities increase ethical responsibility, but they can also produce accountability gaps. When benevolence is presumed, mechanisms for oversight and evaluation are often underdeveloped. Formal governance may be weak, informal authority may be strong, and feedback channels may be ambiguous.

Psychological research on moral identity suggests that individuals strongly identified with being "good" are sometimes less responsive to the evidence of harm. *Jonathan Haidt's* work indicates that moral self-concept can inhibit self-correction by motivating post hoc justification rather than inquiry.

Within occupational psychosis, care identities substitute intention for impact. Harmful outcomes are attributed to complexity, recipient failure, or external resistance rather than system design. Accountability is diffused through appeals to compassion, sacrifice, or limited resources.

This does not imply that care-oriented institutions are inherently harmful. It underscores the necessity of external accountability, reflexive governance, and disciplined language. Without these, moral authority becomes insulation rather than responsibility.

Nonprofit, religious, and meaning-based institutions demonstrate how moral authority and care identities can obscure accountability and suppress dissent. The next chapter examines a different but structurally related context in peer-based occupational ecosystems and entrepreneurial authority.

Chapter 11 explores how authority that is produced through reputation, visibility, and peer validation, rather than formal structure, creates distinct pathways for occupational psychosis to emerge in unregulated professional spaces.

CHAPTER 11

PEER-BASED OCCUPATIONAL ECOSYSTEMS AND ENTREPRENEURIAL AUTHORITY

Peer-based occupational ecosystems, including founder networks, entrepreneurial communities, creator economies, and influence-driven professional spaces, operate under a distinct configuration of authority. Unlike corporate, governmental, or credentialed systems, legitimacy here is socially produced rather than formally granted. Authority emerges through visibility, reputation, affiliation, and perceived success rather than mandate, licensure, or hierarchy.

These ecosystems are often celebrated for their agility and innovation. They can also be uniquely vulnerable to occupational psychosis. In the absence of formal governance, authority is regulated horizontally by peers and vertically by attention. Identity, narrative, and reputation become the primary mechanisms through which reality is interpreted and defended.

11.1 Social Authority Without Formal Governance

In peer-based ecosystems, authority is generated through recognition. Individuals accrue influence by attracting followers, forming alliances, demonstrating confidence, or associating with perceived success. Governance is implicit rather than codified. Norms are enforced through inclusion, exclusion, and reputational signaling. This configuration enables rapid coordination but limits accountability. Without clear scope-of-practice boundaries or oversight mechanisms, authority claims are difficult to evaluate. Legitimacy rests on social proof rather than on standards that are external to the group.

Sociological research has long noted that informal authority systems rely heavily on shared beliefs and mutual reinforcement. *Max Weber* distinguished charismatic authority from rational-legal authority, observing that charisma depends on recognition rather than rule. In contemporary peer ecosystems, charisma is often mediated by platforms and networks rather than by personal presence alone.

Within occupational psychosis, the absence of governance allows distortion to spread laterally. Claims circulate and intensify through repetition and endorsement. Correction is difficult because no recognized authority exists to adjudicate competing narratives. What gains traction is not necessarily what is accurate, but what is socially affirmed.

11.2 Mimetic Identity Inflation and Extraction

Peer-based ecosystems are highly mimetic. Participants observe which identities, language, and narratives receive validation and then they replicate them. While mimicry accelerates learning and belonging, it also facilitates identity inflation. Mimetic identity inflation occurs when individuals adopt amplified versions of occupational identities such as expert, guide, founder, or healer based on observed success rather than on substantive grounding. Identity precedes function. The performance of authority substitutes for its evaluation.

Anthropological and sociological theories of mimesis emphasize how imitation structures social life. *René Girard* argued that desire and rivalry are socially mediated, leading to escalation rather than differentiation. In entrepreneurial ecosystems, mimetic escalation can inflate authority claims while obscuring limits.

Extraction emerges as a downstream effect of mimetic inflation. Language, concepts, and narratives circulate freely and are detached from the origin or accountability. The boundary between learning and appropriation blurs. Distortion is rarely experienced as unethical because imitation is framed as participation and adaptation rather than as misrepresentation.

Within occupational psychosis, mimetic dynamics normalize overreach. Authority claims multiply without corresponding checks, and the ecosystem experiences expansion as vitality rather than as dilution. Correction is resisted because it threatens the shared illusion of legitimacy.

11.3 Reputation as Regulatory Mechanism

Reputation functions as regulation in the absence of formal governance. Visibility, endorsements, and social standing determine who is trusted and who is marginalized. Reputation can incentivize ethical behavior, but it can also entrench distortion when popularity is substituted for accountability.

Reputational systems are inherently reactive. They respond to visible signals of confidence, narrative coherence, and affiliation rather than to the long-term impact. Negative feedback is often indirect, delayed, or socially costly to deliver. As a result, reputational regulation favors surface alignment over substantive correction.

Organizational scholars have shown that reputational concerns can suppress dissent and encourage conformity. *Mark Granovetter's* work on social networks demonstrated how embeddedness shapes behavior through relational dependence. In peer ecosystems, reputational dependence intensifies self-censorship.

Within occupational psychosis, reputation becomes a self-reinforcing loop. Those with visibility attract more affirmation, which is interpreted as validation. This validation consolidates authority. Harm, when it occurs, is reframed as controversy or misunderstanding rather than as evidence requiring examination.

Because reputational systems lack due process, correction often takes the form of sudden exclusion rather than gradual learning. This volatility further discourages reflexivity, encouraging risk-averse conformity instead.

Peer-based occupational ecosystems illustrate how authority can arise without formal structure and how distortion can propagate through social affirmation, mimicry, and reputational regulation. The final chapter of Part III examines unregulated professional and influence-driven fields, where authority claims extend beyond peer communities into markets and public discourse without corresponding oversight.

Chapter 12 explores how ambiguity of scope, credential uncertainty, and influence without accountability create conditions in which occupational psychosis becomes both portable and persistent.

CHAPTER 12

UNREGULATED PROFESSIONAL AND INFLUENCE-DRIVEN FIELDS

Unregulated professional and influence-driven fields occupy a growing portion of contemporary occupational life. These fields operate outside formal licensure, statutory oversight, or unified professional standards, yet they often exert a significant impact on individuals, organizations, and public discourse. Authority in such contexts is derived from visibility, persuasion, and perceived expertise rather than from institutional mandate or credentialed accountability.

This configuration produces a distinct pathway for occupational psychosis. Where authority expands without corresponding oversight, and where legitimacy is socially conferred rather than structurally bounded, distortion can normalize rapidly. The absence of formal constraints does not eliminate power; it reconfigures it, shifting regulation from institutions to perception itself.

12.1 Authority Without Oversight

In unregulated fields, authority is asserted rather than granted. Individuals position themselves as experts, guides, or leaders through narrative, confidence, and social validation. Oversight mechanisms such as codes of conduct, disciplinary processes, or scope definitions are informal, fragmented, or nonexistent.

This absence of oversight reflects not freedom from control, but the absence of correction. Authority claims circulate without systematic evaluation, and consequences for error or harm are inconsistent. Legitimacy is maintained through continuity of audience rather than through adherence to external standards.

Sociological analyses of authority emphasize that regulation shapes not only behavior but perception. *Michel Foucault* observed that power is most effective when it operates invisibly, shaping what is taken as true. In unregulated fields, authority operates through repetition and recognition, making distortion difficult to detect from within.

Within occupational psychosis, authority without oversight allows distorted narratives to stabilize. Claims are rarely falsified. They are simply replaced by newer claims. The system experiences itself as dynamic and innovative while remaining structurally insulated from accountability.

12.2 Credential Ambiguity and Boundary Collapse

Credential ambiguity is a defining feature of unregulated professional fields. Titles, certifications, and qualifications proliferate without shared standards or enforcement. Boundaries between roles, such as educator, advisor, healer, strategist, or advocate blur, which allows authority claims to migrate across domains.

Boundary collapse occurs when distinctions between expertise areas erode. Individuals move fluidly between roles without recalibrating responsibility or competence. The absence of clear scope-of-practice definitions makes it difficult to assess where authority legitimately applies and where it overreaches.

Professional sociologists have noted that boundary maintenance is essential for ethical accountability. *Andrew Abbott* argued that professions are defined not only by knowledge but also by jurisdiction, understood as the recognized limits of authority. In unregulated contexts, jurisdiction is self-declared rather than negotiated.

Within occupational psychosis, credential ambiguity enables identity inflation. Authority is inferred from presentation rather than substantiated grounding. Harm is not experienced as malpractice because there is no shared criteria to define it. The system normalizes overextension as versatility or innovation.

12.3 Ethical Drift Through Normalization

Ethical drift in unregulated fields does not arise from the explicit abandonment of values. It emerges through normalization. Practices that would provoke concern in regulated contexts become routine through repetition, peer affirmation, and audience acceptance.

Normalization operates incrementally. Small boundary crossings go unchallenged, while language softens responsibility and expectations shift. Over time, what was once exceptional becomes standard. Ethical evaluation gives way to market or reputational feedback as the primary corrective mechanism.

Psychological research on normalization shows that repeated exposure reduces sensitivity to deviation. *Philip Zimbardo's* work on situational influence demonstrated how environments shape behavior without requiring conscious intent. In unregulated fields, the environment rewards visibility and certainty rather than restraint.

Within occupational psychosis, normalization stabilizes distortion by making it unremarkable. Harm is reframed as misunderstanding, resistance, or acceptable risk. Correction becomes unlikely because no shared baseline exists against which to measure deviation.

The result is a system that appears to be self-regulating but is in fact self-reinforcing, expanding authority while diffusing responsibility.

Part III has examined how occupational psychosis manifests across diverse authority systems, from corporate, governmental, credentialed, moral, peer-based, and unregulated. Despite their differences, these systems share a common vulnerability in their inability to detect distortion from within.

Part IV turns to this failure directly. It examines why occupational wellness frameworks despite their intent to support human well-being often fail to recognize occupational psychosis, and how prevailing models inadvertently individualize what is fundamentally systemic.

PART IV

WHY OCCUPATIONAL WELLNESS FAILS TO DETECT IT

Parts I-III established occupational psychosis as a systemic phenomenon shaped by role identity, authority, incentives, language, and governance across multiple authority systems. Part IV turns to a paradox in which the very field tasked with safeguarding occupational well-being often fails to recognize this phenomenon.

Occupational wellness has expanded rapidly in response to burnout, disengagement, and workforce instability. Its growth reflects genuine need. Yet its dominant models are frequently oriented toward individual experience rather than occupational structure, emphasizing coping, resilience, and personal adjustment while leaving the architecture of work largely intact.

This section examines how prevailing occupational wellness frameworks, despite their benevolent intent, can inadvertently obscure systemic distortion. They may treat symptoms while leaving the underlying dynamics unexamined by individualizing harm and moralizing adaptation. The result is not the failure of care, but a misalignment of level in which systemic problems are addressed with individual tools.

CHAPTER 13

THE BLIND SPOTS OF OCCUPATIONAL WELLNESS MODELS

Occupational wellness models emerged at the intersection of health promotion, organizational psychology, and human resources. They prioritize the prevention of burnout, the enhancement of engagement, and the support for work-life balance. These goals are legitimate and necessary. However, the conceptual boundaries of many models limit their diagnostic reach.

The blind spots examined in this chapter do not reflect negligence or bad faith. They arise from foundational assumptions about where harm originates and how it should be addressed. When those assumptions remain unexamined, occupational psychosis can persist undetected.

13.1 Individualization of Systemic Harm

A defining feature of contemporary occupational wellness is the individualization of distress. Burnout, disengagement, and moral injury are frequently framed as outcomes of personal stress, insufficient coping capacity, or misalignment between individual needs and job demands.

This framing directs attention toward interventions that are aimed at the individual in the form of stress management, mindfulness, boundary setting, and self-regulation. While these approaches can provide relief, they also reposition systemic harm as personal deficit. Responsibility shifts from system design to individual adaptation.

Scholars of work and health have cautioned against this displacement. *Christina Maslach* emphasized that burnout is fundamentally a relational phenomenon arising from the chronic mismatch between people and their work environments. When interventions focus solely on individual resilience, they risk obscuring the organizational conditions that generate distress.

Within occupational psychosis, individualization has a further consequence in that it renders role-induced distortion invisible. If harm is experienced as personal strain rather than systemic misalignment, the source of distortion remains unexamined. The system appears neutral and the individual appears maladapted.

This dynamic can produce secondary harm. Individuals may internalize failure when wellness strategies prove insufficient, which reinforces guilt or self-blame. Meanwhile, the occupational structures that constrain reflexivity and accountability remain intact.

13.2 Resilience Narratives and Misplaced Responsibility

Resilience has become a central concept within occupational wellness, and it is framed as the capacity to adapt, recover, and persist. Resilience narratives emphasize strength, flexibility, and personal agency. In many contexts, these narratives are empowering. In others, they misplace responsibility.

Resilience narratives become problematic when they imply that enduring harmful conditions is a marker of virtue or competence. Under such framing, those who struggle are perceived as insufficiently resilient rather than as responding appropriately to systemic strain. Adaptation becomes the moral expectation.

Critical scholars have noted that resilience discourse can align too closely with organizational interests. *Eva Illouz* argued that therapeutic language in contemporary culture often individualizes structural problems and encourages emotional management rather than social change. In occupational settings, resilience can function as a buffer that absorbs harm without triggering correction.

Within occupational psychosis, resilience narratives interact with identity and authority to sustain distortion. Individuals are encouraged to adapt to environments that impair reflexivity rather than to question those environments. The absence of distress is taken as evidence of health, even when ethical or systemic harm persists.

This does not negate the value of resilience. It clarifies its limits. Resilience is a human capacity, not a diagnostic tool. When used to explain away systemic harm, it becomes part of the blind spot that it was meant to address.

Chapter 13 has shown how occupational wellness models can individualize systemic harm and misplace responsibility through resilience narratives. The next chapter examines a related limitation, which is the tendency to treat burnout as a root cause rather than as a symptom.

Chapter 14 explores why burnout frameworks, recovery models, and wellness interventions often miss the deeper structural distortions that give rise to occupational psychosis and why symptom relief alone cannot resolve systemic failure.

CHAPTER 14

BURNOUT IS NOT THE ROOT CAUSE

Burnout has become the dominant explanatory frame for distress at work. It is widely measured, widely discussed, and widely addressed through wellness initiatives, recovery programs, and individual interventions. This attention reflects genuine concern. It also reflects a conceptual shortcut.

When burnout is treated as the root cause of occupational harm, the analysis stops at the level of experience rather than proceeding to the level of structure. Occupational psychosis persists precisely because burnout is positioned as the problem to be solved, rather than as a signal pointing beyond itself.

14.1 Burnout as Symptom, Not Source

Burnout is best understood as a syndrome of chronic occupational stress, characterized by exhaustion, cynicism, and reduced efficacy. Decades of research have clarified its contours and consequences. Crucially, this research has also demonstrated that burnout arises from systemic mismatch between people and their work environments, not from individual weakness.

Christina Maslach and colleagues emphasized that burnout reflects enduring misalignment across domains such as workload, control, reward, community, fairness, and values. These mismatches are structural. They are produced by how work is organized, evaluated, and governed.

Treating burnout as a source rather than a symptom reverses this causal logic. Exhaustion becomes the explanatory endpoint rather than the evidence of deeper dysfunction. The question shifts from *what is wrong with the system* to *how can individuals recover.*

Within occupational psychosis, this reversal has significant consequences. Burnout becomes the visible manifestation of harm, while the role-induced distortions that generate it remain unexamined. Attention focuses on depletion rather than on the mechanisms that normalize ethical drift, suppress reflexivity, and insulate authority from correction.

This misattribution also obscures cases in which burnout is absent. Occupational psychosis can persist in environments where individuals remain energized, engaged, and outwardly successful. The absence of burnout is mistakenly interpreted as evidence of health, even when systemic harm is ongoing.

Burnout, then, is neither trivial nor sufficient. It is an indicator that is sometimes loud, and sometimes silent of deeper occupational conditions that require structural analysis.

14.2 Why Recovery Models Miss Structural Distortion

Recovery models within occupational wellness emphasize restoration in the form of rest, resilience, reengagement, and the return to functioning. These models are appropriate for addressing fatigue and strain. They are less effective at detecting structural distortion.

Recovery assumes that the environment to which one returns is fundamentally sound. The goal is to restore capacity so that individuals can resume participation. When the environment itself impairs judgment, ethics, or accountability, recovery becomes recycling by returning individuals to systems that continue to generate harm.

Scholars of work and organizations have noted this limitation. *Richard Sennett* argued that contemporary work arrangements can erode character and coherence even as they reward adaptability. Recovery restores functioning without addressing whether what is being restored is sustainable or ethical.

Within occupational psychosis, recovery models can inadvertently reinforce distortion. By emphasizing adaptation, they align with systems that prioritize continuity over correction. Individuals learn to manage their responses rather than to question the structures shaping those responses.

This dynamic also interacts with authority. Leaders may interpret successful recovery as confirmation that systems are functioning adequately. The reappearance of productivity becomes evidence of organizational health, even when the underlying conditions remain unchanged.

None of this negates the value of recovery. It clarifies its limits as a diagnostic lens. Recovery addresses consequence, not cause. When burnout is treated as the problem to be fixed, occupational psychosis remains unnamed and undetected.

Chapter 14 has shown why burnout and recovery frameworks, while necessary, are insufficient for diagnosing systemic distortion. The next chapter examines a deeper vulnerability, which is the absence of governance within occupational wellness itself.

Chapter 15 explores how wellness initiatives, when they are untethered from scope, ethics, and institutional oversight, can reproduce the very dynamics they seek to address, transforming care into another site of unexamined authority.

CHAPTER 15

WELLNESS WITHOUT GOVERNANCE

Occupational wellness has expanded rapidly in scope, visibility, and influence. Programs, initiatives, and professional roles now operate across organizations, sectors, and authority systems, often with the stated aim of supporting human well-being at work. Yet this expansion has largely occurred without corresponding development of governance structures.

Governance determines who may act, within what boundaries, and under what ethical constraints. In its absence, even benevolent efforts can generate harm. This chapter examines how wellness initiatives, when untethered from scope, ethics, and institutional accountability become vulnerable to occupational psychosis themselves.

15.1 Absence of Scope and Ethics

A defining feature of contemporary occupational wellness is the absence of clearly articulated scope. Wellness roles frequently overlap with leadership development, mental health support, organizational culture, and identity work, yet boundaries between these domains are often implicit or undefined.

Without scope, authority expands by default. Practitioners and programs may address increasingly complex psychological, ethical, or organizational issues without clear mandate or accountability. The distinction between support and intervention blurs, and the distinction between facilitation and influence collapses.

Professional governance literature emphasizes that scope of practice is not a constraint on care, but a condition of ethical action. *Andrew Abbott* argued that professions are constituted by jurisdiction, the socially recognized limits of authority. Where jurisdiction is absent or ambiguous, accountability weakens.

In occupational wellness, ethical frameworks are often aspirational rather than enforceable. Codes of conduct may exist, but they lack mechanisms for oversight, review, or sanction. As a result, ethical responsibility becomes individualized rather than institutionalized.

Within occupational psychosis, this absence of governance allows distortion to normalize. Wellness initiatives may unintentionally reproduce the same dynamics that they seek to mitigate, including role inflation, narrative insulation, and diffusion of responsibility. The system experiences itself as caring while remaining structurally unaccountable.

15.2 Good Intentions as Risk Factor

Good intentions are central to wellness work. They motivate care, reduce stigma, and encourage engagement. They also constitute a risk factor when intention substitutes for evaluation of impact.

Research on moral psychology suggests that strong moral self-concept can inhibit critical self-examination. *Jonathan Haidt* noted that individuals often reason defensively to protect their moral identity. In wellness contexts, the identity of "helper" or "supporter" can discourage scrutiny by framing critique as cynicism or opposition to care.

When good intentions are presumed sufficient, harm becomes difficult to name. Missteps are reframed as learning experiences without corresponding structural correction. The absence of negative feedback is interpreted as success rather than as lack of detection.

Within occupational psychosis, intention-based legitimacy mirrors the dynamics observed in other authority systems. Wellness roles acquire moral insulation, and governance gaps widen. Care becomes an identity rather than a function subject to evaluation.

This does not negate the value of wellness initiatives. It clarifies the necessity of institutional stewardship. Without governance, wellness risks becoming another site where systemic distortion is normalized under the language of care.

Part IV has shown why occupational wellness models often fail to detect occupational psychosis and how, without governance, wellness itself can become structurally vulnerable to distortion. The final section of this volume turns toward implications and responsibility.

Part V examines the cost of leaving occupational psychosis unnamed and the ethical necessity of restraint, governance, and stewardship. It asks not how to intervene, but who is responsible for ensuring that intervention is possible without reproducing harm.

PART V

IMPLICATIONS, BOUNDARIES, AND STEWARDSHIP

The preceding sections have defined occupational psychosis, traced its mechanisms, examined its manifestations across authority systems, and explained why prevailing occupational wellness frameworks often fail to detect it. Part V turns to implications and responsibility.

Naming a phenomenon is not merely an intellectual act. It carries ethical weight. What remains unnamed is rarely governed and what is not governed tends to reproduce itself. This section examines the cost of silence, including the human, organizational, and societal consequences of leaving occupational psychosis undefined and unmanaged, and clarifies why restraint, boundaries, and stewardship are prerequisites for any responsible engagement.

CHAPTER 16

THE COST OF NOT NAMING OCCUPATIONAL PSYCHOSIS

When systemic distortion remains unnamed, it is experienced only through its consequences. Individuals feel strain without explanation; organizations address symptoms without cause; and societies absorb costs without attribution. The absence of language does not neutralize harm, it distributes it invisibly.

This chapter examines the cumulative costs of failing to name occupational psychosis. These costs do not arise from dramatic failure alone; they accumulate quietly through normalization, misattribution, and delayed correction.

16.1 Human Cost

At the human level, the cost of not naming occupational psychosis is borne as confusion, self-blame, and moral injury. Individuals experience distress in the form of burnout, anxiety, cynicism, or disengagement when no framework exists to locate harm within the occupational structure rather than in personal inadequacy.

When systemic distortion is individualized, people internalize failure. They are encouraged to adapt, recover, or become more resilient without being given language to understand why adaptation feels futile or ethically compromising. Over time, this can erode self-trust and agency.

Research on moral injury underscores this dynamic. Moral injury arises when individuals are placed in situations that violate deeply held values without the power to correct the conditions that produce that violation. While the concept has been studied extensively in military and healthcare contexts, its relevance extends to any occupational system that constrains ethical reflexivity. As *Jonathan Shay* observed, moral injury is less about exposure to trauma than about betrayal by authority structures.

Within occupational psychosis, individuals may continue to function effectively while experiencing a growing dissonance between their values and actions. Without language to name the source, this dissonance is misinterpreted as personal weakness or failure to cope. The human cost is not only exhaustion, but loss of moral coherence.

16.2 Organizational Cost

Organizations that fail to name occupational psychosis incur costs that are often misattributed or delayed. These include chronic turnover, disengagement, reputational erosion, and repeated cycles of reform that address surface symptoms while leaving underlying dynamics intact.

When distortion is normalized, organizations invest in corrective initiatives, such as training, wellness programs, and cultural interventions, without addressing the structures that generate harm. The result is initiative fatigue, the repeated effort with diminishing returns. Trust erodes as employees perceive that problems are acknowledged rhetorically but left structurally unchanged.

Organizational scholars have noted that learning fails when systems interpret success as confirmation rather than as a prompt for inquiry. *James G. March* emphasized that organizations often learn more from failure than from success, yet systems that deny or defer recognition of harm deprive themselves of that learning.

Occupational psychosis compounds this loss by insulating decision-makers from corrective signals. As reflexivity collapses, organizations become less adaptive precisely when adaptation is most needed. The cost is not only inefficiency, but institutional brittleness, a reduced capacity to respond ethically and strategically to changing conditions.

16.3 Societal and Economic Cost

At the societal level, the cost of not naming occupational psychosis manifests as misallocated resources, diminished public trust, and escalating economic burden. When systemic harm is treated as individual pathology, solutions are directed toward treatment rather than prevention, and recovery rather than redesign.

Economic analyses of work-related stress and disengagement consistently demonstrate substantial productivity loss and healthcare expenditure. Yet these figures capture only the most visible costs. Less visible are the opportunity costs, including innovation foregone, ethical capacity depleted, and civic trust eroded.

Sociologists of modern institutions have warned that systems which cannot see their own effects generate unintended consequences at scale. *Ulrich Beck* described how contemporary societies produce risks that outpace their capacity to recognize and manage them. Occupational psychosis represents such a risk, one that is diffuse, normalized, and structurally obscured.

When authority systems repeatedly fail to correct themselves, public confidence weakens. Institutions appear disconnected from lived experience, and legitimacy erodes. The economic cost is compounded by a social one through a loss of faith in the capacity of work and leadership to serve human well-being.

Chapter 16 has outlined the cumulative costs of leaving occupational psychosis unnamed. The next chapter turns to boundaries, specifically why this volume stops at definition and why restraint is an ethical act rather than a limitation.

Chapter 17 examines the dangers of premature application and clarifies the conditions under which responsible engagement with this concept can occur without reproducing the very distortions it seeks to illuminate.

CHAPTER 17

WHY THIS BOOK STOPS AT DEFINITION

This volume has argued that occupational psychosis is a systemic phenomenon requiring careful naming, conceptual clarity, and institutional responsibility. It has also deliberately stopped short of application. This decision is neither incidental nor provisional. It reflects an ethical position grounded in the risks of premature use and the responsibilities that accompany definitional authority.

In fields that shape identity, authority, and well-being, the move from concept to application is not neutral. Without governance, scope, and oversight, even accurate diagnoses can become instruments of distortion. This chapter explains why restraint is necessary and why definition is itself a substantive contribution.

17.1 The Danger of Premature Application

Applying a concept before its boundaries are established carries predictable risks. When definitions circulate without governance, they are easily instrumentalized and used to legitimize authority, justify intervention, or extract value without accountability.

History offers numerous examples of psychological and organizational concepts that were widely adopted before their ethical implications were understood. In such cases, language intended to clarify harm became a tool for categorization, control, or moral judgment.

The problem was not the concept itself, but the absence of institutional discipline governing its use.

Scholars of science and knowledge production have cautioned against this dynamic. *Michel Foucault* emphasized that concepts do not merely describe reality; they participate in its organization. Once a term enters practice, it reshapes power relations by determining who may name, interpret, and act.

Within occupational psychosis, premature application would replicate the very dynamics the concept seeks to illuminate. Labeling systems, roles, or individuals without reflexive constraint risks moralization rather than diagnosis. It collapses systemic analysis into attribution, inviting misuse in contexts lacking ethical safeguards.

Stopping at definition therefore functions as a protective boundary. It preserves conceptual integrity while preventing unauthorized extension into domains where harm could be amplified rather than reduced.

17.2 Restraint as an Ethical Act

Restraint is often misinterpreted as omission or limitation. In ethical inquiry, restraint is a positive act because it is a decision to withhold power until responsibility structures are in place.

Ethicists and organizational scholars have noted that authority without restraint tends toward overreach. *Hannah Arendt* warned that the failure to think critically about the consequences of action, especially within role-bound systems, enables harm through normalization rather than intent. Restraint interrupts this process by slowing action in favor of reflection.

In the context of occupational wellness, restraint counters the prevailing pressure to produce tools, frameworks, and interventions rapidly. It acknowledges that concepts addressing identity, power, and ethics require institutional stewardship, not individual improvisation.

By stopping at definition, this book affirms that not all knowledge should be immediately actionable. Some knowledge serves a different function in that it names, clarifies, and creates conditions under which responsible action might later occur. This is particularly true where application would require training, oversight, and ethical governance beyond the scope of a single text.

Restraint also signals respect for those affected by occupational psychosis. It refuses to treat lived experience as a testing ground for ungoverned intervention. Instead, it insists that care precedes control, and that authority be matched by accountability.

If restraint defines the boundary of this volume, governance defines the path forward. The final chapter turns from limitation to responsibility, examining what ethical governance in occupational wellness would require and why institutional stewardship, rather than individual initiative, is the necessary condition for any future engagement with occupational psychosis.

CHAPTER 18

TOWARD ETHICAL GOVERNANCE IN OCCUPATIONAL WELLNESS

This volume has argued that occupational psychosis is not a failure of intent, compassion, or expertise, but a failure of structure. Where authority expands without reflexive constraint, where identity fuses with role, and where language substitutes for accountability, distortion becomes normalized. The question that remains is not how to intervene, but what must be in place before intervention can occur responsibly.

The answer is governance.

Governance does not resolve harm directly. It establishes the conditions under which harm can be seen, named, and addressed without reproducing the distortions that made it invisible in the first place.

18.1 Governance as Prerequisite for Care

Care without governance is vulnerable to overreach. It may be well-intentioned, but it lacks the structural discipline necessary to prevent ethical drift. Governance is therefore not an administrative afterthought; it is a prerequisite for ethical care.

Governance defines boundaries by clarifying who may act, within what scope, under what standards, and with what accountability. It distinguishes support from authority, diagnosis from judgment, and care from control. In professional fields, governance protects both those who offer care and those who receive it.

Sociological scholarship has long emphasized that professions are constituted not merely by expertise, but by jurisdiction and oversight. As *Andrew Abbott* argued, authority without jurisdiction collapses into ambiguity, and ambiguity undermines accountability. Where scope is undefined, responsibility diffuses and harm becomes difficult to contest.

In occupational wellness, the absence of governance has allowed roles to expand laterally into domains of identity, meaning, leadership, and ethics without corresponding safeguards. This expansion has not been malicious; it has been structural. Yet without governance, care risks becoming indistinguishable from influence, and support from authority.

Governance introduces friction intentionally. It slows action, requires justification, and demands reflexivity. In doing so, it protects care from becoming coercive and prevents ethical certainty from substituting for ethical responsibility.

18.2 Institutional Responsibility and the Future of the Field

Occupational psychosis cannot be resolved through individual insight alone. Because it arises within systems, responsibility for its governance rests at the institutional level. This includes organizations, professional bodies, educational institutions, and any entity that authorizes, legitimizes, or scales occupational wellness practices.

Institutional responsibility begins with acknowledgment. It requires recognizing that wellness initiatives, leadership development, and care-oriented roles are not neutral interventions but forms of authority. Once authority is acknowledged, governance becomes unavoidable.

Political theorists have warned that authority that is unexamined tends toward normalization of harm. *Hannah Arendt* emphasized that ethical failure often arises not from intent but from the collapse of thinking within role-bound systems. Governance restores thinking by embedding reflection, accountability, and limitation into structure.

The future of occupational wellness depends not on innovation alone, but on institutional maturation. This maturation requires moving beyond individualized solutions toward governance frameworks capable of holding systemic complexity. It requires resisting the pressure to act before boundaries are defined, and to scale before stewardship is secured.

Occupational psychosis names a threshold. It marks the point at which occupational wellness must decide whether it will remain a collection of well-intentioned practices or evolve into a governed field capable of ethical responsibility.

CONCLUSION: FROM INVISIBLE HARM TO INSTITUTIONAL RESPONSIBILITY

This volume has defined occupational psychosis to make visible a form of systemic distortion that has long operated without language. It has shown that harm within occupational systems does not require malice, incompetence, or psychological disorder. It arises instead from the convergence of role identity, authority, incentive structures, professional language, and the absence of reflexive governance.

Across corporate, governmental, healthcare, nonprofit, peer-based, and unregulated professional contexts, the same pattern recurs in which occupational systems maintain internal coherence while losing contact with the external consequences of their actions. Distortion becomes normalized. Ethical drift is reframed as necessity. Responsibility diffuses until harm appears nowhere and everywhere at once.

Occupational psychosis names this condition without moralization and without diagnosis. It shifts attention away from individual failure and toward institutional design. It clarifies why burnout, disengagement, and moral injury persist despite widespread wellness initiatives, and why recovery without governance cannot resolve systemic harm.

This book stops at definition by design. It offers no methods, frameworks, or interventions, not because the problem is insoluble, but because premature application would reproduce the very dynamics this work seeks to expose. Definition is not an absence of action, but a prerequisite for responsible action.

If occupational wellness is to mature as a field, it must develop the capacity to examine its own authority structures, ethical assumptions, and governance gaps. Naming occupational psychosis is a step toward that capacity. What follows must be institutional, bounded, and governed.

The work of stewardship begins where certainty ends.

EPILOGUE

After the Name Is Given

This book has not argued that work is pathological, nor that people are broken. It has argued something quieter and more unsettling in that systems can distort perception without announcing themselves as distortions, and that harm can emerge not from malice, but from unexamined roles operating at scale.

Occupational Psychosis is not a condition to be cured. It is a pattern to be recognized.

Once named, it cannot be unseen.

The danger addressed here does not lie in ignorance, incompetence, or bad intent. It lies in normalization, when incentives replace judgment, when roles eclipse identity, and when ethical responsibility is diffused across structures until no one feels accountable for outcomes that nonetheless persist.

Modern work has become extraordinarily effective at producing motion, metrics, and meaning narratives. It has been less effective at producing reflection proportional to its power. In that imbalance, distortions take hold quietly, often celebrated as success.

This volume has served one purpose, which is to draw a boundary where none previously existed.

What follows this boundary is how institutions respond, whether governance evolves, and whether responsibility is reclaimed, which does not belong to this book. That work requires deliberation, stewardship, and structures capable of holding complexity without collapsing into simplification or exploitation.

The absence of solutions here is not an omission. It is restraint.

In systems where everything demands optimization, restraint is itself a form of care.

If this book leaves the reader with discomfort rather than closure, that is appropriate. Discomfort signals contact with reality before it has been reorganized into something easier to carry. The task of this work has been to interrupt certainty, not replace it.

Occupational Psychosis does not end with a call to action. It ends with a call to attention.

What happens next belongs not to a method, a market, or a movement, but to the quality of discernment we are willing to bring back into the places where work, power, and identity quietly converge.

REFERENCES

Chapter 1

Arendt, H. (1963). *Eichmann in Jerusalem: A report on the banality of evil.* Viking Press.

Bandura, A. (1999). Moral disengagement in the perpetration of inhumanities. *Personality and Social Psychology Review, 3*(3), 193–209. https://doi.org/10.1207/s15327957pspr0303_3

Foucault, M. (1980). *Power/knowledge: Selected interviews and other writings, 1972–1977* (C. Gordon, Ed.). Pantheon Books.

Janis, I. L. (1982). *Groupthink: Psychological studies of policy decisions and fiascoes* (2nd ed.). Houghton Mifflin.

Luhmann, N. (1995). *Social systems.* Stanford University Press.

Maslach, C., & Leiter, M. P. (2016). Understanding the burnout experience: Recent research and its implications for psychiatry. *World Psychiatry, 15*(2), 103–111. https://doi.org/10.1002/wps.20311

Schein, E. H. (2010). *Organizational culture and leadership* (4th ed.). Jossey-Bass.

Weick, K. E. (1995). *Sensemaking in organizations.* Sage Publications.

Zimbardo, P. G. (2007). *The Lucifer effect: Understanding how good people turn evil.* Random House.

Chapter 2

Arendt, H. (1963). *Eichmann in Jerusalem: A report on the banality of evil.* Viking Press.

Bandura, A. (1999). Moral disengagement in the perpetration of inhumanities. *Personality and Social Psychology Review, 3*(3), 193–209. https://doi.org/10.1207/s15327957pspr0303_3

Milgram, S. (1974). *Obedience to authority: An experimental view.* Harper & Row.

Schein, E. H. (2010). *Organizational culture and leadership* (4th ed.). Jossey-Bass.

Weick, K. E. (1995). *Sensemaking in organizations.* Sage Publications.

Chapter 3

Arendt, H. (1963). *Eichmann in Jerusalem: A report on the banality of evil.* Viking Press.

Bandura, A. (1999). Moral disengagement in the perpetration of inhumanities. *Personality and Social Psychology Review, 3*(3), 193–209. https://doi.org/10.1207/s15327957pspr0303_3

Janis, I. L. (1982). *Groupthink: Psychological studies of policy decisions and fiascoes* (2nd ed.). Houghton Mifflin.

Keltner, D., Gruenfeld, D. H., & Anderson, C. (2003). Power, approach, and inhibition. *Psychological Review, 110*(2), 265–284. https://doi.org/10.1037/0033-295X.110.2.265

Schein, E. H. (2010). *Organizational culture and leadership* (4th ed.). Jossey-Bass.

Chapter 4

Campbell, D. T. (1979). Assessing the impact of planned social change. *Evaluation and Program Planning, 2*(1), 67–90.

Edmondson, A. C. (2018). *The fearless organization: Creating psychological safety in the workplace for learning, innovation, and growth.* Wiley.

Senge, P. M. (2006). *The fifth discipline: The art and practice of the learning organization* (Rev. ed.). Doubleday.

Weick, K. E., & Sutcliffe, K. M. (2015). *Managing the unexpected: Sustained performance in a complex world* (3rd ed.). Wiley.

Chapter 5

Edmondson, A. C. (2018). *The fearless organization: Creating psychological safety in the workplace for learning, innovation, and growth.* Wiley.

Keltner, D., Gruenfeld, D. H., & Anderson, C. (2003). Power, approach, and inhibition. *Psychological Review, 110*(2), 265–284. https://doi.org/10.1037/0033-295X.110.2.265

Schein, E. H. (2010). *Organizational culture and leadership* (4th ed.). Jossey-Bass.

Weick, K. E., & Sutcliffe, K. M. (2015). *Managing the unexpected: Sustained performance in a complex world* (3rd ed.). Wiley.

Chapter 6

Bourdieu, P. (1991). *Language and symbolic power.* Harvard University Press.

Foucault, M. (1980). *Power/knowledge: Selected interviews and other writings, 1972–1977* (C. Gordon, Ed.). Pantheon Books.

Haidt, J. (2012). *The righteous mind: Why good people are divided by politics and religion.* Pantheon Books.

Illouz, E. (2007). *Consuming the romantic utopia: Love and the cultural contradictions of capitalism.* University of California Press.

Weick, K. E. (1995). *Sensemaking in organizations.* Sage Publications.

Chapter 7

March, J. G. (1991). Exploration and exploitation in organizational learning. *Organization Science, 2*(1), 71–87. https://doi.org/10.1287/orsc.2.1.71

Kunda, G. (2006). *Engineering culture: Control and commitment in a high-tech corporation* (Rev. ed.). Temple University Press.

Schein, E. H. (2010). *Organizational culture and leadership* (4th ed.). Jossey-Bass.

Weick, K. E., & Sutcliffe, K. M. (2015). *Managing the unexpected: Sustained performance in a complex world* (3rd ed.). Wiley.

Chapter 8

Arendt, H. (1963). *Eichmann in Jerusalem: A report on the banality of evil.* Viking Press.

Darley, J. M., & Latané, B. (1968). Bystander intervention in emergencies: Diffusion of responsibility. *Journal of Personality and Social Psychology, 8*(4), 377–383. https://doi.org/10.1037/h0025589

Scott, J. C. (1998). *Seeing like a state: How certain schemes to improve the human condition have failed.* Yale University Press.

Weber, M. (1978). *Economy and society* (G. Roth & C. Wittich, Eds.). University of California Press.

Chapter 9

Freidson, E. (2001). *Professionalism: The third logic.* University of Chicago Press.

Illich, I. (1976). *Medical nemesis: The expropriation of health.* Pantheon Books.

Institute of Medicine. (2000). *To err is human: Building a safer health system.* National Academies Press.

Kuhn, T. S. (1962). *The structure of scientific revolutions*. University of Chicago Press.

Timmermans, S., & Berg, M. (2003). *The gold standard: The challenge of evidence-based medicine and standardization in health care*. Temple University Press.

Chapter 10

Arendt, H. (1963). *Eichmann in Jerusalem: A report on the banality of evil*. Viking Press.

Durkheim, É. (1912/1995). *The elementary forms of religious life* (K. E. Fields, Trans.). Free Press.

Haidt, J. (2012). *The righteous mind: Why good people are divided by politics and religion*. Pantheon Books.

Selznick, P. (1957). *Leadership in administration: A sociological interpretation*. Harper & Row.

Weber, M. (1978). *Economy and society* (G. Roth & C. Wittich, Eds.). University of California Press.

Chapter 11

DiMaggio, P. J., & Powell, W. W. (1983). The iron cage revisited: Institutional isomorphism and collective rationality. *American Sociological Review, 48*(2), 147–160. https://doi.org/10.2307/2095101

Girard, R. (1977). *Violence and the sacred*. Johns Hopkins University Press.

Granovetter, M. (1985). Economic action and social structure: The problem of embeddedness. *American Journal of Sociology, 91*(3), 481–510. https://doi.org/10.1086/228311

Weber, M. (1978). *Economy and society* (G. Roth & C. Wittich, Eds.). University of California Press.

Chapter 12

Abbott, A. (1988). *The system of professions: An essay on the division of expert labor.* University of Chicago Press.

DiMaggio, P. J., & Powell, W. W. (1983). The iron cage revisited: Institutional isomorphism and collective rationality. *American Sociological Review, 48*(2), 147–160. https://doi.org/10.2307/2095101

Foucault, M. (1980). *Power/knowledge: Selected interviews and other writings, 1972–1977* (C. Gordon, Ed.). Pantheon Books.

Zimbardo, P. G. (2007). *The Lucifer effect: Understanding how good people turn evil.* Random House.

Chapter 13

Illouz, E. (2007). *Consuming the romantic utopia: Love and the cultural contradictions of capitalism.* University of California Press.

Maslach, C., & Leiter, M. P. (2016). Understanding the burnout experience: Recent research and its implications for psychiatry. *World Psychiatry, 15*(2), 103–111. https://doi.org/10.1002/wps.20311

Rose, N. (1999). *Governing the soul: The shaping of the private self* (2nd ed.). Free Association Books.

Sennett, R. (1998). *The corrosion of character: The personal consequences of work in the new capitalism.* W. W. Norton & Company.

Chapter 14

Maslach, C., & Leiter, M. P. (2016). Understanding the burnout experience: Recent research and its implications for psychiatry. *World Psychiatry, 15*(2), 103–111. https://doi.org/10.1002/wps.20311

Schaufeli, W. B., Leiter, M. P., & Maslach, C. (2009). Burnout: 35 years of research and practice. *Career Development International, 14*(3), 204–220. https://doi.org/10.1108/13620430910966406

Sennett, R. (1998). *The corrosion of character: The personal consequences of work in the new capitalism.* W. W. Norton & Company.

Chapter 15

Abbott, A. (1988). *The system of professions: An essay on the division of expert labor.* University of Chicago Press.

Haidt, J. (2012). *The righteous mind: Why good people are divided by politics and religion.* Pantheon Books.

Rose, N. (1999). *Governing the soul: The shaping of the private self* (2nd ed.). Free Association Books.

Sennett, R. (2006). *The culture of the new capitalism.* Yale University Press.

Chapter 16

Beck, U. (1992). *Risk society: Towards a new modernity.* Sage Publications.

March, J. G. (1991). Exploration and exploitation in organizational learning. *Organization Science, 2*(1), 71–87. https://doi.org/10.1287/orsc.2.1.71

Maslach, C., & Leiter, M. P. (2016). Understanding the burnout experience: Recent research and its implications for psychiatry. *World Psychiatry, 15*(2), 103–111. https://doi.org/10.1002/wps.20311

Shay, J. (2014). *Moral injury.* Psychoanalytic Psychology, 31(2), 182–191. https://doi.org/10.1037/a0036090

Chapter 17

Abbott, A. (1988). *The system of professions: An essay on the division of expert labor.* University of Chicago Press.

Arendt, H. (1963). *Eichmann in Jerusalem: A report on the banality of evil.* Viking Press.

Foucault, M. (1980). *Power/knowledge: Selected interviews and other writings, 1972–1977* (C. Gordon, Ed.). Pantheon Books.

Chapter 18

Abbott, A. (1988). *The system of professions: An essay on the division of expert labor.* University of Chicago Press.

Arendt, H. (1963). *Eichmann in Jerusalem: A report on the banality of evil.* Viking Press.

Foucault, M. (1980). *Power/knowledge: Selected interviews and other writings, 1972–1977* (C. Gordon, Ed.). Pantheon Books.

Sennett, R. (2006). *The culture of the new capitalism.* Yale University Press.

CITATION GUIDANCE

This work is intended to be cited as a conceptual, diagnostic, and analytical text, not as a methods manual or applied intervention guide.

Recommended Citation (APA 7th Edition)

Arts, G. L. (2026). *Occupational psychosis: The hidden crisis beneath occupational wellness.* Occupational Wellness Institute.

Notes for APA users:

- Capitalize only the first word of the title and subtitle, and proper nouns.
- Italicize the book title.
- Cite this work as conceptual and analytical in nature.

Recommended Citation (Chicago Manual of Style, 17th Edition)

Notes and Bibliography Format

Arts, Georgia Lee. *Occupational Psychosis: The Hidden Crisis Beneath Occupational Wellness.* United States: Occupational Wellness Institute, 2026.

Author-Date Format

Arts, Georgia Lee. 2026. *Occupational Psychosis: The Hidden Crisis Beneath Occupational Wellness*. United States: Occupational Wellness Institute.

Notes for Chicago users:

- Use headline-style capitalization for the title and subtitle.
- Location may be omitted if not required by the journal or institution.
- Cite this work as a foundational diagnostic text.

CANON INDEX

Occupational Wellness Institute Canon

Arts, Georgia Lee
Occupational Psychosis: The Hidden Crisis Beneath Occupational Wellness Designated canonical volume. Diagnostic and definitional in scope; non-operational.

Pre-Canonical Works by the Author

The following works were published prior to the formal establishment of the Occupational Wellness Institute Canon. They are governed independently and do not carry canonical designation.

Arts, Georgia Lee
The $2 Trillion Revenue Gap™ How Identity Misalignment Is Silently Costing America Trillions and How Identity Alignment Transforms People, Workplaces, and Communities Applied analysis written for public, organizational, and policy audiences.

Arts, Georgia Lee
Dream Journey, Breaking the Dream Barriers™ A Guide to Bridging Identity Gaps in Life and Career. Conceptual and narrative work exploring identity, meaning, and personal inquiry.

ABOUT THE AUTHOR

Georgia Lee Arts is the founder and steward of the Occupational Wellness Institute™. Her work focuses on occupational wellness, identity alignment, ethical governance, and the systemic conditions that shape modern work, leadership, and institutional life.

With a background spanning military service, organizational leadership, human development, and scholarly inquiry, Arts brings a systems-level lens to questions often addressed only at the individual or symptomatic level. Her work examines how roles, incentives, and professional structures influence perception, judgment, ethics, and identity, frequently in ways that remain invisible within conventional wellness and leadership paradigms.

Arts' writing is characterized by a deliberate separation between definition and application, emphasizing conceptual clarity, ethical restraint, and institutional responsibility. Her canonical work contributes to emerging discourse at the intersection of occupational psychology, organizational behavior, identity science, and governance.

She resides in the United States and continues to develop scholarly and institutional work through the Occupational Wellness Institute™

www.ingramcontent.com/pod-product-compliance
Lightning Source LLC
LaVergne TN
LVHW051051210926
848486LV00002B/69